India
A Photographic Journey

India
A Photographic Journey

John Gallagher

**BARNES
& NOBLE**

NEW YORK

M 10 9 8 7 6 5 4 3 2 1

ISBN 0 7607 7335 1

Editor: Don Gulbrandsen
Design: Danny Gillespie/Compendium Design

Printed in China through Printworks Int. Ltd.

Acknowledgments

Arcaid: 2, 8, 9, 13, 17, 20, 22, 24, 28, 31. **Fotolibra:** 148T, 171T; David Knowles 7, 38, 40, 41B, 43T, 56 (both), 64, 71T, 78, 79, 84, 85; Peter Armstrong 10; Peter Herbert 12, 158, 159, 164, 166, 167, 171B, 172B, 174, 176, 178, 180, 184, 192; Mervyn Benford 14; Paul Gapper 18; Tom Hoad 26, 118, 120, 121, 130; Magdalena Mayo 30, 71B; Michel Conreur 34, 41T; Robert Wyatt 54, 150; Paul Gapper 80; Philip Hodkinson 162, 172T; Suzannah Conreur 170; Matthew Smith 182 (both). **Corbis:** Reuters/Corbis 1; Lindsay Hebberd/Corbis 4, 32, 48T, 50, 82, 88, 97, 104, 107, 116, 122, 126T, 138, 148B; Macduff Everton/Corbis 6, 36 (both), 39, 108, 112B; Galen Rowell/Corbis 42T, 112T; Sheldan Collins/Corbis 42B; David Samuel Robbins/Corbis 43B, 48B, 76B, 92T; Julian Calder/Corbis 44; John and Lisa Merrill/Corbis 46; Craig Lovell/Corbis 49; Bennett Dean, Eye Ubiquitous/Corbis 52; Jeremy Horner/Corbis 57, 65, 66, 76T, 94, 100, 173; Yann Arthus-Bertrand/Corbis 58, 74; Rob Howard/Corbis 60T; Michael Freeman/Corbis 60B, 154; Tibor Bognár/Corbis 61, 133, 168; Brian A. Vikander/Corbis 62, 67, 72, 113, 114; Wolfgang Kaehler/Corbis 68, 175; Arvind Garg/Corbis 70, 102T; David Cumming, Eye Ubiquitous/Corbis 77, 96B, 106T; Janez Skok/Corbis 86; Chris Hellier/Corbis 90; Christopher Cormack/Corbis 92B; Ric Ergenbright/Corbis 93; Jayanta Shaw/Reuters/Corbis 96T, 103; Roman Soumar/Corbis 98; Abbie Enock, Travel Ink/Corbis 102B; Chris Lisle/Corbis 106B, 134, 140, 152, 160, 185, 186, 190; Earl & Nazima Kowall/Corbis 110; Archivo Iconografico, S.A./Corbis 119T, 145; Barnabas Bosshart/Corbis 119B, 126B, 127, 128; Geoffrey Taunton, Cordaiy Photo Library Ltd./Corbis 124; Tiziana and Gianni Baldizzone/Corbis 132T, 136; Theo Allofs/Corbis 132B; Alamany & E. Vicens/Corbis 142; Richard A. Cooke/Corbis 144, 151; Catherine Karnow/Corbis 149; Martin Jones/Corbis 146; The Cover Story/Corbis 156; Hans Georg Roth/Corbis 188; Bob Krist/Corbis 189.

PAGE 1: Appearing frequently in artworks across the subcontinent, the glorious peacock is the national bird of India.

PAGES 2–3: The muted colors of the subcontinent are dusty ochres, earthy colors spiced with splashes of brighter tones. Rajvilas, an Oberoi Hotel, in northern India at dusk.

RIGHT: A Banyan tree shrine near Dibrugarth. The tree shrine is hung with hundreds of brass bells. The Banyan tree has religious significance for Hindus because of its longevity.

Contents

Introduction

With more than four thousand years of written history, an array of dozens of major cultures, and contacts stretching from Western Europe to East Asia, India's story includes almost every conceivable human experience and way of life. Glamorous Bollywood *filmi* stars and well-heeled computer programmers rub shoulders with devout ascetics and humble farmers. Scorching deserts and snowcapped mountains coexist with teeming cities and tranquil villages. Visitors to this country find themselves in the twenty-first century and the world of the Mughals at the same time. The rich contrasts of Indian life find their roots in a history that is so resilient that it refuses to ever become the mere past.

Prehistoric India

India has been inhabited since the Paleolithic, or Old Stone Age. Hand axes and other archaeological finds have been recovered from early hominid sites at Hathnora in Central India, and the Kalagdi Basin in Southern India. The evidence of mitochondrial DNA research suggests that the ancestors of modern Homo sapiens spread eastwards from Africa toward East Asia and Australasia along the coastline of the Indian subcontinent. The archaeological record still has major gaps, but rock painting dating from 50,000 to 40,000 years ago broadly supports the findings of recent genetics. The World Heritage site of Bhimbetka in Madhya Pradesh represents a later development in Indian Stone Age culture. More than six hundred rock shelters are decorated with vivid rock paintings depicting hunting, dancing, household life, and other scenes.

The Neolithic Period and the Indus Valley Civilization

Neolithic cultures developed early in what is now Pakistan, with the Mehrgahr farming culture up and running in Baluchistan by the seventh millennium B.C. Recent findings suggest that this agricultural society may have started forming up to two millennia earlier, which would put the area at the very forefront of human advancement at that time. The full Neolithic revolution of agriculture, early cities, and evolving states was clearly in full swing by 2800 B.C. By this point, a settled urban culture had arisen in the Indus Valley, centered on the cities of Harappa and Mohenjodaro. These identically planned sites had populations in the range of 30,000 people, and governments that kept records using a pictographic writing system with strong similarities to early Sumerian script from Mesopotamia. The cities were laid out on a grid pattern and built in brick, with multi-storey buildings. The people were fed by a complex system of cereal agriculture that used the waters of the Indus River as a source for widespread irrigation. The social system was equally complex, with a small elite class of religious hierarchs ruling over a population of craftsmen and farmers. Unfortunately, it is not possible to get a close-up look at this culture, because no literature from the period survives. But the surviving artifacts prove beyond doubt that it was a true urban culture. A statuette of a Harappan dancer would not be out of place on MTV. She stands proudly with one hand on her hip, the epitome of urban chic and hauteur. On a more pious note, the religious practices of the time formed the first roots of what was later to grow into Hinduism.

At its height, Indus Valley culture spread over an area including the Valley itself, the western end of the Ganges valley, Gujarat, and northern Afghanistan.

ABOVE: In Sikkim, Buddhist prayer flags have faded in the sun and made ragged by the winds blowing over Dzongri Ridge on Mount Kanchengjunga, the world's third highest mountain.

The language or languages spoken by the Indus peoples is still a topic of debate, and pictographs offer no information on the spoken language they represent. Nevertheless, the consensus view is that the Indus valley culture probably spoke a Dravidian tongue. Dravidian is the family of languages, including Tamil, now mainly confined to the south of the Indian subcontinent. This theory was backed up by the discovery of Brahvi, a surviving Dravidian language in Baluchistan. The Indus Valley's trading network spread far and wide, with boats plying the route all the way to Mesopotamia via the Persian Gulf. Just what was worth sending over such long distances is open to conjecture, but ivory is a prime candidate—the Syrian elephant was by this time long extinct.

Establishing the reasons for the decline of the Indus Valley cities around 1800 B.C. is much more controversial. It's clear that Harappa and Mohenjodaro met a sudden end; the point of debate is exactly who was responsible. Traditionally, the finger of suspicion pointed to the Aryans, a group of warrior tribes speaking an early Indo-European language. But the Aryan invasion theory is open to increasing doubt. Urban civilizations have collapsed under the weight of their own ecological folly—as was the case in Mesoamerica —and many historians of India would prefer that this were the case here also (thus eliminating the need for foreign intervention). From a western viewpoint, the very name "Aryan" has a deeply disturbing ring to it, thanks to the adoption of these tribesmen as the *ubermenschen* (or "blond beasts" in Nietzsche's phrase) of racist fantasy. Still, the existence of Indo-European languages over most of modern northern India suggests that there must have

been a movement of people from the north at about this time. But the weight of evidence increasingly points to continuity as well as disruption. The newcomers did not arrive in a single barbaric flood of chariots and slaughter, and they were definitely influenced by the existing peoples they found. A first major group made its way into the north and west around 2000 B.C., with a further movement across the entire north of the country around 1400 B.C. From this point on, we can speak of a society in which the Sanskrit language was becoming dominant in northern India. This development opens the next stage in Indian history, known as the Vedic.

Vedic Culture

The newcomers brought with them kings, war bands, and legends, and they established a new tribal culture as they settled along the Indus River Valley, then across the Thar Desert and down the valley of the Ganga (Ganges) River.1 Their sacred literature was inscribed in the Vedas, which give their name to the period. Their language, Sanskrit, was understood to be sacred in and of itself.

The Indo-Aryans established the *rashtra* (state) led by the *rajan*, or king. He was assisted by a *senani*, a strategist and army chief who also provided divine protection through charms and oracles. The commoners lived nomadic, cattle-herding lives, though they increasingly settled down as their population grew and agriculture reasserted its importance. The Indo-Aryans also brought the concept of caste to India, where it has persisted to this day. Society was divided into four classes: Brahmin (priests and scribes), Kshatriva (warriors), Vaishya (farmers), and Shudra

BELOW: The Zebu or brahminy cattle are associated by Hindus with the god Siva. As such they are given the freedom to roam where they please—over roads, around towns, and across railroad lines as the mood takes them. They are native beasts to India and in color are usually gray or white, with a large shoulder hump, long dangling ears, and a heavy dewlap.

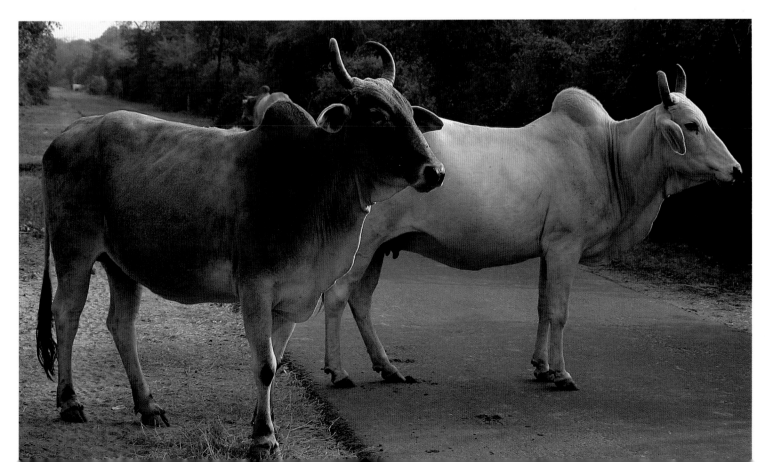

(workers). Those outside this structure were called *adivasis*. For the first few centuries, these castes remained permeable by talent and chance. But they hardened into rigid hereditary categories as society settled down and the early Vedic religion evolved into Hinduism.

Vedic religion had much in common with Zoroastrianism in Persia, with which it shared an Indo-Iranian background. Fire was the sacrificial medium of ritual and the god of fire, Agni, was worshipped along with Indra, Soma, Varuna, Surya (the sun), Vayu (the wind) and the goddesses Ushas (the dawn) and Prithvi (the Earth). River worship was also an integral part of Vedic religion, as were early forms of yoga and asceticism.

The earliest strain of Vedic culture is preserved in the *Rigveda*, a collection of hymns that was almost certainly composed by 1500 B.C. The literature was preserved and expanded under the kingdom of the Kurus, which flourished to the north of the Thar Desert around 1200 B.C. The *Upanishads* were written as the center of Indic political power shifted eastwards to the Pancala kingdom in the Ganga (Ganges) valley three hundred years later.

The epic *Mahabharata* and *Ramayana* were composed after the Vedic period ended around 500 B.C., and the north and east of India coalesced into sixteen *mahajanapadas* or Great Kingdoms. By this time, a new wave of foreign invaders was streaming into the Indus Valley, under Darius I, Emperor of Persia. The Persians found a sophisticated civilization in India that was well on the way towards developed Hinduism.

Hinduism

Properly known as *Sanatana Dharma* or the Eternal Faith, Hinduism is a sum of the religious beliefs developed among historical communities all throughout India, including the classical Indus Valley cultures as well as the Indo-Iranian elements of the population. As such, the religion has no founder and no single organizational core, though the Vedic and post-Vedic scriptures are generally accepted as authoritative. The Hindu triad of major divinities and multitude of local cult figures presented European observers with a severe cultural headache: Is the faith polytheistic (worshipping many gods), monotheistic (believing in a single supreme god), or Trinitarian (worshipping one god in three persons)? In fact, Hinduism is none of the above—it's henotheistic, meaning that it recognizes one deity, Brahma, and accepts other gods and goddesses as aspects or manifestations of the Supreme Being. "The truth is One, but different sages call it by different names," goes the traditional, tolerant Hindu saying.

The ultimate object of Hindu worship, then, is Brahma, the Creator who never ceases to create. The other members of the main triad are Vishnu, the

ABOVE: City Palace was built for Raja Sawai Jai Singh II almost as a city within a city when he built Jaipur. The magnificent palace is an architectural mixture between elaborate Rajput detailing and open and airy Mughal styles.

RIGHT: Another ornate palace in Jaipur is the Hawa Mahal (Palace of the Winds). It was built in 1799 for the ladies of the royal household so that they could enjoy the fresh air while remaining in purdah. Accordingly, despite its imposing facade, most of the building is only one room deep.

Preserver—who upholds and protects the Creation under a number of guises including Krishna—and Shiva the Destroyer—destructive, erotic, and compassionate all at once. Local divinities are worshipped in the villages, and some (like the elephant-headed god Ganeshi or Ganesh) are accepted throughout entire regions. In the main urban areas, Vaishnavaism lays more stress on the worship of Vishnu while Shivaism emphasizes devotion to Shiva. Other tendencies within the faith blend both forms.

The main Hindu beliefs include *samsara.*—the transmigration of the soul through a cycle of death and rebirth. Rebirth into a higher or lower state is determined by karma, the accumulated weight of one's good and evil deeds. The ultimate goal of religious life is liberation from this cycle of *samsara.*

The ethics of Hinduism are based on four doctrines. In everyday life, the most important of these is *dharma*, the achievement of righteousness in one's way of life. The fulfillment of legitimate material and sensual needs is defined as *artha* and *kama* respectively. The final aim in life, called *moksha*, is ultimate liberation from the cycle of worldly rebirth, and it takes precedence for those who have abandoned the world and its desires. It can be seen in action in modern India when respectable businessmen abandon their secular lives on retirement to go wandering as homeless holy men. Yoga forms the basis of the long tradition of achieving *moksha* through meditation, and the ascetic strain in Hinduism is a similar (and sometimes extreme) attempt to abandon the worldly mind through control of the earthly body.

Finally, it is important to note that Hinduism does not recognize any distinction between religion and other aspects of life. Everything from diet, working life, and social class to political beliefs are parts of a seamless whole for practitioners of the faith. With the exception of a few recently founded groups, Hinduism does not seek to convert others to its beliefs. One is born rather than become a Hindu.

Buddhism

Buddhism developed as a reform movement within Hinduism, partly in reaction to the established faith's increasing reliance on ascetic practice and its acceptance of a rapidly hardening caste system. The religion shares much ground with Hinduism, but there are also striking differences. The first of these is that Buddhism has a historical founder.

Siddhartha Gautama was born to a princely clan called the Shakyas in 560 B.C., in what is now southern Nepal. Legend has it that he grew up within the royal enclosure carefully shielded from witnessing sickness, old age, or death. His first sight of aged, sick, and dead people disturbed him so profoundly that he

embarked on a quest for understanding, leaving his family and life of luxury at the age of 29. He spent time with gurus, and for five years practiced a regime of such extreme self-denial that his fellow-ascetics became his followers. Again, he failed to find the answers he was seeking. He was shaken out of this lifestyle by the casual kindness of a peasant girl, who offered the starving Siddhartha some food; his followers deserted him when he accepted it. Finally, at the age of 35, he resolved to sit in meditation under a *bodhi* tree in the town of Bodh Gaya until he had attained truth. Around dawn one May morning, he realized his goal, and became the Buddha, the "One who is Awake." The remainder of his long life until the age of eighty was spent teaching the truths he had realized, and establishing a religious community. His first sermon was held in a deer park in the city of Sarnath, near Benares, an event known as "setting the wheel of teaching in motion."

The fundamental Buddhist teachings are contained in two sets of precepts called the Four Noble Truths and the Eightfold Path. The Four Noble Truths are: that life involves suffering; that suffering arises from attachment to desires; that suffering ceases when attachment to desire ceases; and that freedom from suffering is attainable through the principles set out in the Eightfold Path. The Eightfold Path consists of Right Viewpoint, Right Thinking, Right Speech, Right Action, Right Livelihood, Right Effort, Right Mindfulness and Right Contemplation. The central concerns of Buddhism are evolved from those of Hinduism, and face the same human dilemmas—most notably, the question of release from the cycle of death and rebirth, and escape from worldly illusion.

Egalitarianism was a driving force in the spread of Buddhism. The primary Buddhist religious community was known as the *sangha*, and was open to all men irrespective of birth status. During the Buddha's own lifetime, membership of the *sangha* was opened to women also—at the insistence of his aunt and wife. The first ordained Buddhist monk, Upali, had been a barber in his earlier life. Within the *sangha*, he was accepted as a senior even over nobles who joined the ranks later. No other community in India at the time offered anything like this openness.

Shortly after the Buddha's death, his followers gathered in council at Rajagrha (Rajagira, Bihar) and formally agreed on an accepted version of the founder's teachings. The unity of Buddhist belief only lasted for about a century, however. A second council held at Vaishali split into conservative and pro-reform camps. The reformers broke away calling themselves the Mahasangha, or "great community of believers." This was the origin of the Mahayana (or so-called Greater Vehicle) tradition in Buddhism, which was

to dominate in northern Asia. The conservative grouping at Vaishali grew into the Sthaviravada or "Way of the Elders" tradition, which spread as far as Sri Lanka and developed a range of distinct Buddhist schools. The most influential doctrine among these was Sri Lankan Theravada Buddhism, which became highly influential in Southeast Asia. The paradox is that though Buddhism became one of India's outstanding influences on the outside world, its home region was eventually reabsorbed almost completely into Hinduism, or incorporated into the Islamic world.

Jainism

Jainism, or *Jain Dharma*, was another religious movement that grew out of the Hindu world during the sixth century B.C. Its founding figure is a prince named Mahavira (599-527), though the religion claims historical roots reaching back to Mohenjodaro and Harappa. The central concerns of Jainism are shared with the other two major Indian schools of thought, i.e., release from *samsara*, or the reincarnatory cycle. Jainism has many distinctive teachings,

ABOVE: The first glimpse of the Taj Mahal never fails to impress. The entire complex became a UNESCO World Heritage site in 1983. The Taj is located in the city of Agra and sits amid four acres of gardens and ornamental trees beside the River Jamuna.

however, including a complex cyclical view of history and a commitment to nonviolence. Jainism does not believe in the idea of a creator god; the universe is uncreated and eternal, though not unchanging. It passes through a cycle of six successive stages, during the last of which even knowledge of Jainism itself will be lost. (We are presently in the fifth stage of the cycle.) Then the process begins over again; knowledge of religious truth is once again recovered, and the process repeats itself infinitely.

The non-violent principles of Jainism commit believers to strict vegetarianism—which is not always the case in Hinduism, despite popular misconceptions to the contrary. Out of respect for all living things, stricter Jains may wear masks over their mouths to prevent harming small insects through breathing. Jainism's resolute nonviolence was an important influence on the development of Gandhi's thinking. On the whole, Jainism stayed closer to the ascetic cast of Hindu practice than Buddhism did, though the two younger religions originated in a close relationship with each other.

Jainism is widely spread over the Indian subcontinent, but its main concentrations are in New Delhi, Maharashtra, Rajathstan, and Gujarat. With about four and a half million followers, this is a relatively small community in India, but its members have had a cultural influence well above their numbers. The Jain faith is sometimes confused with another remarkable minority community, the Parsees. They are, however quite distinct. The Parsees are an Indian branch of Zoroastrianism, the religion of the ancient Persian Empire. They survive in very small numbers in Mumbai (Bombay) and a few other cities.

Greek Invasions

Meanwhile, back in the fifth century B.C., an obscure state called Macedon launched itself onto the world stage under a young generalissimo known to history as Alexander the Great. The only enemy that could really satisfy him was Persia, the world superpower of the age. He demolished it in a series of lightning campaigns that brought him to the Indus Valley in 326 B.C. The Greeks were astonished to come across naked ascetics who were completely immune to threats and unafraid of death. They called them the "gymnosophists" or naked philosophers. Alexander was more than willing to launch yet another campaign down the Ganga Valley, but his exhausted troops had had enough. They staged a sit-down strike, and refused to budge until their leader marched them home.

Buddhism Ascendant: The Mauryan Empire

Most of India paid little attention to Alexander's exploits on the northwestern fringes of the country. Elsewhere in northern India, a new power was on the move—the Mauryan Empire, expanding under its ruler Chandragupta (who reigned from 324 to 301 B.C.). From their capital at Pataliputra (near modern-day Patna in Bihar), Mauryan forces surged the length and breadth of the Ganga valley. They created India's first major centralized empire, the first real rival to the ancient political sophistication of Harappa and Mohenjodaro. The capital boasted markets, temples, libraries, and a university. There were registered foreigner communities, and even licensed red-light districts.

The trade network spread as far as Alexander's empire (now busy splitting up after his death). The administration covered provinces and districts right down to village level. This was a thoroughly regulated society. One of the masterminds of the whole enterprise was the Brahmin Kautilya, author of a remarkable work called *The Science of Material Gain*. The book is a clear-eyed, unsentimental, and quite amoral how-to book on running an empire, feeding an army, and nourishing the government coffers— Bollywood it ain't.

Chanragupta's grandson Ashoka is one of the great figures of Indian history. In his early years (he reigned from 269 to 232 B.C.) he was a normal, busy imperialist, ruling a domain from modernday Afghanistan to Bangladesh—and he fought hard to expand his empire. However, he had a change of heart when he witnessed an attack on the kingdom of Kalinga (now Orissa). He was so disgusted by the slaughter that he renounced war for the rest of his life. Ashoka devoted his reign to righteousness, non-violence, and religious tolerance. He set up his guiding principles on stone monuments across the empire, written out in local languages. While he respected all religions, Ashoka was a devout Buddhist, and the Mauryan Empire became the stage for a great expansion of Buddhism.

The Greeks, Again

Alexander's army had followed (or rather pushed) their leader back home, but the Greeks never forgot about India. As the Mauryan Empire decayed in the second century B.C., they seized their chance to make a comeback, invading from the Hellenistic kingdom of Bactria in Afghanistan and Central Asia. The country was an isolated splinter of Alexander's original empire, but the Greco-Bactrians were far from parochial. Their position on the Silk Road put them in touch with cultures from Egypt to China. As they pressed down the Ganga Valley, they rapidly adopted Indian culture as well. By 175 B.C., they were in control of the Punjab, Gujarat, and the Ganga basin as far as Patna. And they were fast becoming Indo-Greeks—Buddhist and multilingual, ruled by a king named Demetrius who wore an

BUDDHA

Buddha was born two and a half thousand years ago in ancient India some time around 560 B.C., at Lumbini (now in Nepal) in the lower Himalayas. Little is known for certain about his life but the legend goes as follows. His father was Suddhodana, king of the Sakhyas, who gave his son the name Siddhartha Gautama. Astrologers predicted he would become a great leader or to his father's great concern, a monk. To avert the latter Siddhartha was protected from knowledge of the outside world and instead given every possible luxury. At age 16 he married princess Yashodhara who bore him a son named Rahula. At about the age of 29 Siddhartha escaped the confines of the palace and was shocked at the poverty all around him. He immediately renounced the luxuries of the material world, shaved his head, and donned saffron robes. For six years he lived among, and learned from, hermits and holy men, and led a life of extreme austerity. In the process, he grew so weak that he almost starved to death. One day, after settling under a large Bodhi tree (the Tree of Wisdom) at Bodhgaya (now Bihar in North India), he meditated for a long time until he reached the state of Nirvana (self-enlightenment). Then he danced in divine ecstasy for seven days and nights around the great tree. Increasingly known as Buddha, he left to travel the world to teach others wisdom and enlightenment through the Four Noble Truths so they, too, could achieve Nirvana. He died at about the age of 80 in the village of Kusinagari (now Kasia).

ABOVE: The Indian elephant for centuries was essential to many aspects of Indian life. Although now outmoded by machines for many of their uses, elephants are still employed as working animals in the jungle and fields as well as having a role in numerous temple celebrations and public festivals, all of which they seem to enjoy. Unfortunately, Asian elephants are now an endangered species.

north, Dravidian society was matrilineal and much less stratified, though Brahmins were accorded high respect. In other ways, though, the area was part of a broader Indian whole. The Vedic religion percolated south along with Sanskrit elite culture, and Hinduism, Buddhism, and Jainism were all accepted here also. Dravidians were active traders and travelers. A network of sea lanes connected them with the Mediterranean, along with Myanmar and Southeast Asia. Roman gold coins and artifacts have been discovered in the area. As Southeast Asia developed its own trading networks, southern Indian culture became a driving force in the shaping of the region's identity.

The major Tamil kingdoms of Chera, Chola, and Pandya constantly battled for control in the south, while simultaneously developing an impressive vernacular literature. Further north in the Deccan (the southern Indian peninsula), the Satavahana kingdom flourished from the third century B.C. to the first century A.D. Its structure and culture were modeled on the Mauryan Empire, and it played an important role as a transmitter of new cultural influences from north to south.

Hinduism Resurgent: The Gupta Empire

Northern India finally regained political unity thanks to the rise of the Gupta Empire (A.D. 320 to 550). The main achievement of the empire, centered on Patna, was a long peace. This allowed the development of Hindu culture in its classical form—for although the Guptas were tolerant patrons of Buddhism, the older form of worship made a dramatic comeback during this period.

Hindu religious practice took on the form it retains today, with local and sectarian deities complementing worship of Brahma, Vishnu, and Shiva. The Buddha was also accepted into the Hindu canon as a manifestation of Vishnu. Education and research reached highly developed levels under the empire, with particular advances in astronomy and mathematics. The decimal number system was developed and later passed on to the west by the Arabs. And the Gupta Empire gave us nothing—the very useful null quantity known as zero. Sanskrit literature and medicine also surged ahead. Of all the many empires that came and went during the course of Indian history, none (including the British) was to leave such a permanent mark on the soul of the nation.

The nomads of Central Asia remained busy. From around A.D. 500, a renewed series of attacks began—this time from the Hunas, the Indian version of the White Huns. The Gupta Empire tottered. The strongman Harsha Vardhana (reigned 606-647) cobbled together a brief successor state, but it was not to be. India collapsed into a patchwork of competing kingdoms. The south gained in importance, yet at

elephant crown complete with tusks to symbolize the cultural fusion.

The Indo-Greeks were cultural fusion artists to a rare degree, and their lasting influence was artistic rather than political. Architecture and sculpture in particular were subject to Indo-Greek influences, which were absorbed into the wider stream of Indian traditional styles. The Gandhara style is an especially noteworthy school in this regard. In their religious policy, Buddhism was favored, especially under King Menander, who ranks with Ashoka as one of the great benefactors of Indian Buddhism.

The decline of the Indo-Greek world was complete by about 10 B.C. The prime suspects are Central Asian nomadic powers, some known only by names given to them by Chinese historians. The Sakas, Kushans, and Yue-zhi galloped into the past in quick succession.

The Dravidian South

The Dravidian south continued on it own distinctive course. In contrast to the patriarchal Indo-European

the same time became more assimilated to standard Sanskrit-Hindu cultures. Hindu sectarian devotional movements spread the worship of Shiva and Vishnu, and Buddhism and Jainism declined in importance because of their vigorous efforts. Major literatures developed in all the main Dravidian languages—Tamil, Kannada, Telugu, and Mayalam. Among the more famous masterpieces of the age are *The Jeweled Anklet* and *The Jeweled Belt*, along with a reworking of the ancient *Ramayana* epic in the local Tamil vernacular. These were all important cultural developments in their own right. But the overall political picture after the fall of the Guptas is one of relative drift. The next major impetus towards change was to come from Islam.

The Early Islamic World and India

Considering its explosive growth in the Middle East, North Africa, and Central Asia, Islam was relatively slow to spread in the Indian subcontinent. Contacts were established quite early. An expedition commanded by Muhammad bin Qasim was dispatched by Damascus in 711, and he took control of Baluchistan and Sind. From there Muslim holy men (Sufis) fanned out across the countryside. These men were perhaps the most persuasive teachers of Islam, for their individual piety and simple lives were instantly understandable to a population used to Hindu hermits and ascetics (*saddhus*). Moreover, the respect afforded to the religious scholars of Islam (the *ulema*) was familiar for Hindus, who were long accustomed to the clerical Brahmin caste.

But major Muslim expansion in India had to wait for Islam's second wind, which was provided by the manpower and fighting spirit of the newly converted Turkic-speaking peoples of Central Asia. They commonly entered the core Islamic areas as slaves and elite troops, and soon found that they really were indispensable—so indispensable, in fact, that they took over the whole show. Under the names of Seljuks, Mamelukes, and Ottomans, they created a storm within the Islamic world, toppling long-established thrones and establishing new ones. At the same time, these peoples, under the names of Ghurs and Mughals, were responsible for a major spread of Islam beyond its Middle Eastern heartland. India was a prime theater of conquest.

The Sultanate of Delhi and the Vijayanagara Empire

The decisive launch from the Khyber Pass down the Ganga Valley was accomplished by the Afghan

BELOW: The Law Courts at Chennai (formerly known as Madras), in Tamil Nadu. Chennai was founded and named Fort St. George in 1639 as the first British East India Company settlement in India. The highest minaret on the court building used to be a lighthouse which helped mariners guide their ships into port from the Bay of Bengal.

warlord Muhammed of Ghor in the late 1100s. One of his generals, Qutb-ud-din Aybak, proclaimed himself ruler of the Sultanate of Delhi, the first substantial Muslim Indian state. This Sultanate soon came under Turkic control (like most of the Islamic world at this time.) The result was a characteristic mix of external expansion and internal instability. The Sultanate's armies waged one successful campaign after another. By the 1200s, Bengal and most of the Deccan were under Delhi's control, and the extreme south of the country was briefly conquered in the early 1300s. Being Sultan of Delhi meant being a man of enormous prestige and power, but the job did not come with a pension. During the reigns of the Sultanate's five dynasties up to the sixteenth century, fewer than half of the sultans died in their beds.

More significantly, new social realities were being created on the ground throughout India, especially in the north. Like Buddhism before it, the egalitarianism of Islamic life offered an alternative to the caste system, and this was one of the factors in the acceptance of Muslim rule by many ordinary people. Conversions were numerous, and a new landscape of mosques, madrasas (religious schools), and Sufi memorials emerged alongside the Hindu and Buddhist heritage. New agricultural methods, irrigation schemes and canal building helped revitalize farming, and the highly developed Persian traditions of art and literature played an important role in the development of a local Islamic culture. Major new trade links were established with the Middle East, and metal-working, stone working and textiles all reaped the benefit. But at the same time, the Delhi Sultanate failed to establish an orderly system of internal administration. Local generals and governors were in practice almost independent of the capital, and much of their time was spent positioning themselves for the next *coup d'etat*. They tended to tax the townspeople and peasants under their control greedily.

Meanwhile in the south, the Vijayanagara Empire emerged as the dominant Hindu power from the 1330s. It looked to the ancient Tamil kingdom of Chola for inspiration. Centered in modern Karnataka, its capital, the "City of Victory" was a rich merchant center adorned with magnificent temples, the most important of which was dedicated to Virupaksha, a manifestation of Shiva, patron goddess of the empire.

The Vijayanagara Empire's dominion reached as afar as Goa in the west and Chennai (Madras) in the south, and at times it also controlled areas along the east coast. Commercial guilds played an important part in the political and cultural life of the empire. Commerce increased in importance after Vasco de Gama broke the Arab monopoly of Indian Ocean trade, and the Portuguese established a base at Goa in 1510.

The Vijayanagaran state lasted from 1336 to 1565. For most of its existence, it found itself pitted against the nearest Muslim power to the north, the Bahmani Sultanate of the Deccan. This state was the scene of a notable fusion of Islamic and Hindu art styles. But conflicts between immigrant and convert Muslims and other groups were a constant feature of life. The Bahmani Sultanate collapsed in 1527, giving rise to the five Deccan Sultanates—which between them caused the downfall of Vijayanagara in 1565.

By the sixteenth century, India had received an infusion of Islam that was decisive to the creation of the culture as we now know it. Yet the subcontinent was torn apart by conflict, and its development was slowed by governments that were ineffective when weak and oppressive when strong.

Another set of power shifts in Central Asia now brought about the rise of the final strong central government before the advent of the East India Company and British power over the subcontinent. This was the Mughal Empire.

BELOW: Dawn mist over the Taj Mahal.

The Mughal Empire

Babur of Ferghana was a local ruler in what is now Uzbekistan, a Central Asian leader who claimed descent from the nomadic greats, Genghis Khan and Tamberlaine. Pushed south to the Kabul Valley, he decided to try his hand further south again, in the seething political cauldron of the northern Indian plains. He succeeded against Lodhis, Rajputs, and Afghans. His kingdom, based in Agra and then Delhi, entered history as the Mughal Empire. (Mughal, or Moghul, is a variant of Mongol.) By the time of his death in 1530, the Mughals were expanding as rapidly as the old Sultanate of Delhi, and the Guptas before them. However, they also faced a question that had challenged foreign invaders since as long ago as the age of the Greeks—to what extent should the new ruling class adapt itself to the existing Indian cultures?

This question was especially pressing for Islamic states, because the ruling classes could not simply switch over to the majority religion as the Indo-Greeks, for example, had done. Almost all Islamic empires had to deal with non-Muslim majority subject populations at some stage of their development. And they all developed a similar range of policies to cope, from the Ottomans in the Balkans to the Mughals in the Ganga Valley. Religious tolerance was extended to the subject population. This was in stark contrast to the expanding Christian empires. The unfortunate citizens of Goa, for example, were subjected to the full rigors of the Inquisition on suspicion of heresy and "paganism."

However, religious tolerance in Islamic states did not usually translate into full political equality. Islamic states were governed under sharia law, and non-Muslim subjects paid special discriminatory taxes, known as the *jizya*. Muslim rulers had to tread a fine line between including as many groups as possible among their supporters and offending the more conservative members of their base, who strongly believed that the reins of power in an Islamic state should be firmly held by Muslims alone. The Mughal Empire was remarkable for the range of different ways in which it tried to square the circle.

Akbar (who reigned 1556-1605) was the third in the line of Mughal emperors. His solution to the problem of running an expanding multi-religious empire was tolerance. He permitted the construction of temples, the practice of non-Muslim pilgrimages, and he brought an end to discriminatory taxation in 1564 then he went a step further. In 1580, he propounded a civic religion called Din-i-Ilahi, or the Divine Faith. This new religion was open to all loyal subjects of the empire, regardless of their ethnic background, and the practice of it did not rescind the believer's original faith. (A similar kind of syncretic religion was tried by the Egyptian Caliphate in the eleventh century; it survives today as the Druze faith in the Lebanon.) The extraordinary measure was an attempt to forge a single community of Hindu and Muslim, Sunni and Shia. Naturally, it failed. Those Hindus who had not abandoned their traditional beliefs for Islam were hardly likely to do so now for a newfangled state-sponsored faith. And the pious Sunni Muslims around the throne were scandalized and deeply offended. A policy meant to unite the empire proved to be a prime cause for disunity and eventual downfall.

Akbar was far more successful on the administrative side of things. Warlordism and high taxes had been the bane of the first Delhi Sultanate, and here Akbar went for the jugular. His Afghan-Turkish military officers were paid in cash, not grants of land. And they never got their fingers near the till—taxes were collected by an entirely separate bureaucracy.

Promotion in the administration as well as in the army was entirely dependant on talent and results rather than birth and status. Both spear-carriers and pencil-pushers were personally responsible to the emperor himself, and they were stationed where he told them and for how long. Very few early modern empires were quite so streamlined.

Good government doesn't always create great art (e.g., consider Switzerland in contrast to Italy) but it worked for the Mughals. Architecture and painting in particular thrived, and a vibrant school of miniature painting created a distinctive Indian version of what had originally been a Persian art form. The Mughal dynasty's architects also gave us *the* symbol of India today. The Taj Mahal was constructed as a memorial to Mumtaz Mahal, the beloved second wife of the emperor Shah Jahan. Her death during childbirth in 1631 so devastated the emperor that (legend has it) his hair turned white overnight. Part of a larger complex of mosques and gardens, the mausoleum poses and answers the fundamental concerns of Islamic architecture in a stunning *tour de force.*

Shah Jahan's successor, Aurangzeb (who reigned 1658-1707) presided over the decline but not the fall of the Mughal Empire. Not that it seemed in decline on the surface, for under his reign the empire reached its greatest extent ever. In fact, Aurangzeb took on the title Alamgir—or "Seizer of the World." But there were two problems. The first was imperial overreach, and the second was rigid thinking. The empire became so militarized that there was not enough cash to pay the generals, and land was substituted as a reward for victory. This destroyed one plank of Akbar's policies, absolute control of the military aristocracy. Secondly, Aurangzeb was more pious than wise. Determined to put Sunni Islam into a position of unchallenged supremacy in the state, he reintroduced the discriminatory taxes on non-

CLIVE OF INDIA

Robert Clive (1725-1774) was born in 1725 near Market Drayton in Shropshire into a respectable—but not particularly well off—land-owning family. After an undistinguished school career (but one in which he had already proved himself ambitious and contentious), Clive was sent to Madras as a clerk in the East India Company. He was 18 years old, and it was a time when the British and French were fighting for control of the subcontinent. Initially Clive hated India and suffered fits of depression. In 1746 Clive was commissioned as an ensign in the British Army. In the midst of a constantly fluctuating and tense political situation he came to the forefront in 1751 by defending Fort Arcot for 53 days with minimal men and supplies. At 27 he became a hero. In 1753 he returned to England for two years, then was sent back to India by the East India Company as governor of Fort St David and commissioned as a lieutenant-colonel in the army. He resumed a distinguished military career, including recapturing Calcutta from the Nawab of Bengal, and defeating the Nawab in the Battle of Plassey. For three years Clive effectively ruled Bengal for the company. In 1760 he returned to England as a very rich man, became a member of parliament, and was made Baron Clive of Plassey. In 1764 he again returned to India as governor and commander-in-chief of Bengal. He stayed for three years, but on his return to England was accused of corruption. In 1773 his name was cleared, but he nevertheless committed suicide in November 1774.

Muslims in 1679. This destroyed the other plank of Akbar's government, relative religious tolerance. It was more than the empire could bear, and revolts broke out in the north and in the Deccan. The Deccan in particular was the scene of intense guerilla fighting over two decades, and the cost to Mughal prestige was immense. The fighting also wrecked the agricultural economy of large parts of the empire, causing many subjects who might otherwise have stayed loyal to start questioning where their best interests lay. The Mughals limped on for another century longer, but their glory days were done.

Mughal Decline

Resistance to Mughal domination came from a number of quarters, both within India and from outside. The brave guerilla fighters of the Deccan were known as the Marathas. Originally mercenary fighters for the Muslim sultans of Bijapur, they took advantage of the warfare between their employers and the Mughals to carve out a kingdom of their own, with its capital at Pune. From there, these Hindu upstarts became the scourge of the Mughals, launching raids of pillage and plunder deep into imperial territory.

The Maratha leader was the charismatic Shivaji Bhonsle (1627-1680), and his war cry was for the restitution of Hinduism in India. His arch-foe Aurangzeb was merely "Seizer of the World"; Shivaji went one better, proclaiming himself "Lord of the Universe" in 1674. He immediately started making good on this claim, relieving the Mughals of his home province of Maharashtra, along with Orissa and Bengal. The Mughals asked for peace in 1717; the Marathas signed the treaty and just kept advancing. The problem was that the long years of banditry left them with bad habits they could not break. The never made the transition from looters to genuine liberators. And they retained their mercenary state of mind, happily serving their former Mughal enemies as hired swords against the marauding Afghans. A bloody defeat at their hands in 1761 put an end to the Marathas' streak of good luck. Their kingdom broke up into five squabbling "statelets."

Another source of resistance came from the Punjab, in the shape of a new religious movement, the Sikhs. The Sikh religion is a syncretic blend of Hinduism and Islamic beliefs. The core elements are closer to Hinduism, but the Sikhs abandoned the caste system from the very beginning of their faith in the fifteenth century. As the empire weakened, they seized their chance for independence, and took over the bulk of northwest India during the 1770s. Their loose confederation then expanded into Kashmir and Afghanistan. The Sikhs proved themselves tolerant, brave, and tenacious. The Mughals and Marathas now live on only in the history books,

while the Sikhs are still a formidable presence in twenty-first century India.

One final opponent who outlasted the Mughals was the Nizam (viceroy) of Hyderabad. The first of the line, Asaf Jah, decided he'd had enough of being just a viceroy in 1724, and started a line of independent Nizams that stretched in hereditary succession all the way to the formation of a federal republic in 1948.

European Power in India

The gradual decay of the Mughal Empire provided Europeans with the perfect opportunity to entrench and expand their position in India. In the original colonial division of the world into western and eastern spheres of influence—controlled by the Portuguese and Spanish respectively—India fell to the Portuguese. In 1510, they took control of the island of Goa, where they remained for four and a half centuries. By the beginning of the following century, the northern European states were ready for their turn at world domination. The English East India Company was incorporated in London in 1600, and the Dutch replied with the *Verenigde Oost-Indische Compagnie*—or United East India Company—two years later.

Despite their later start, the Dutch had better fortunes during their early forays in India. In 1609, they set up a fortified trading post about 12 miles north of Chennai, at Pulicat. Their astonishing trade network stretched all the way from New Amsterdam to Nagasaki, and their Indian stations supplied slave labor for their plantations in the East Indies. The English acquired their first foothold on the subcontinent in 1619, at Surat in Gujarat. Other European states followed. The French *Compagnie des Indes Orientales* set up shop in Puducheri (Pondicherry) in the 1660s, and the Danes followed in the 1690s with "factories" near Kolkata (Calcutta, also called Kolkota) and Patna. Even the Austrians got in on the act in the 1720s, near Surat. The various Indian rulers were quite happy to play host to these often-barbarous and greedy merchant companies. They were merely new players in an already crowded field, and could be pitted at will against other Indian rulers or each other. The Europeans offered cash, trade opportunities, and advanced weapons technology in return for cooperation from the Indians.

The East India Company

From their original base in Surat, the East India Company began to build up a chain of trading posts along the coasts of India. Fort Saint George was built at Chennai in 1639, and factories (trading posts) followed in a string of other locations, of which the most important were Kolkata and Mumbai (now Bombay). These early successes, along with the obvious weakening of the Mughal Empire, led to a premature overconfidence on the company's part. The English decided to take on the severe and pious Aurangzeb in 1688, and suffered a severe mauling at his hands in the three years of war that followed. However, the Mughal Empire was now too weak to push its advantage, and the following decades saw a steady rise in the company's power and profits.

Three presidencies were established based on the three major company towns. The merchants settled in fortified "White Towns," with local populations living in "Black Towns" half a mile or so away. While frequently racist, this was not an apartheid society. The company merchants frequently intermarried with the locals, learned the languages (Persian especially, it being the *lingua franca* of the time) and many of them settled down for life in India. The rising power of the company a compared to the empire was demonstrated in 1717, when the Mughal administration waived its right to collect customs duties from the English in Bengal. But the company's real glory days were only beginning.

In 1743, an obscure Englishman by the name of Robert Clive arrived in India in the company's employ. He soon switched over from the company's administrative branch to its military arm, led by British officers and staffed by Indian mercenaries known as sepoys. Clive made something of a name for himself during his ten-year stint, and returned to England a wealthy man. While he was busy enjoying his newfound wealth, war broke out between France and Britain—a world war, with theaters of battle in North America and Asia as well as Europe. The fighting weakened the Europeans' overall position in India. Siraj-ud-daulah, the Nawab (or prince) of Bengal, took the opportunity to seize the East India Company's base at Kolkata in 1756. The fall of the town generated one of the most notorious controversies in Anglo-Indian history—the "Black Hole of Calcutta."

The story goes that 146 men, women and children of Kolkata's English community were taken prisoner and crammed into a dank, windowless dungeon in the citadel of Fort William. There they were left untended overnight. In the morning, when the door was opened, only twenty-three survivors emerged. The survivor John Holwell wrote up an incendiary account of the affair, which inflamed public opinion back home. Intense controversy has surrounded the incident ever since. It has been pointed out that the dungeon, measuring eighteen by twenty-four feet, could not have conceivably held the numbers cited by Holwell, however crushed the prisoners had been. Historians sympathetic to the cause of Indian freedom have argued that he must have exaggerated his account significantly. Others have insisted that his entire story was a fabrication

from beginning to end. Certainly there are no corroborating accounts to back it up. A figure of sixty-nine people seems closer to the truth, and it is unlikely that the Nawab was involved.

In the greater scale of things, however, it makes no difference whether Holwell was telling the truth or not. The story was widely believed in England and was taken as proof that the Indians were irredeemably cruel and depraved, as opposed to the civil and virtuous British. The Black Hole proved to its highly self-serving audience that India needed the British to save them from themselves.

ABOVE: Steps at the Jantar Mantar, the largest of the five Observatories built by Jai Singh II in the early eighteenth century. Built between 1718 and 1734 Jantar Mantar was restored in the late nineteenth century. The arched door is made from red sandstone and white marble. This is part of the small equitorial sundial placed on the local meridian line.

In its hour of crisis, the company called on Robert Clive to return to India and get the situation back on track. Clive was more than willing to go back; he left a failed political career and a string of unsatisfied creditors in his wake. Arriving in Chennai in 1756, he gathered his forces and moved on to Bengal, where he succeeded in retaking Kolkata. A showdown with Nawab Siraj-ud-daulah was inevitable. The two armies met on June 23, 1757, at the village of Palashi (Plassey), between Kolkata and Murshidabad.

Part of Clive's genius as a commander was that he thoroughly understood the nature of the war he was fighting. In a contest of mercenary armies, nothing speaks louder than money. Clive bribed many of the Nawab's soldiers, and when the company's artillery opened fire the opposition largely laid down their weapons and surrendered with little fighting. Siraj-ud-daulah was not helped by the presence of a turncoat in his ranks who desired his position—Mir Jafar swung the formations under his command over to the company's side, joining their comrades who'd already been bought. The whole thing was over in a couple of hours. The company had survived and triumphed in Bengal.

By the time the war with France ended in 1763, the company had also triumphed in the hinterland of Madurai, installing their man as ruler against the French candidate. Clive was now ready to take on the Mughals directly. In 1765, he defeated the emperor Shah Alam at Baksar (Buxar) in Bihar. The victory won a dramatic settlement for British interests in India. The company received the right to administer and tax Bengal, Bihar and Orissa. The nature of the political landscape was instantly and permanently changed. The East India Company was no longer an association of merchant traders. It was a power in the land, ruling over the destinies of twenty-five million subjects.

Robert Clive was intelligent enough to take the power for himself and leave the day-to-day governing to others. The Nawab of Bengal remained the Nawab, and he in turn paid annual tribute to the Mughal Emperor. Nothing much had changed according to this polite fiction. The reality was colder and quite different. The company ruthlessly exercised its newly won authority to collect taxes in Bengal, and started bleeding the province dry. Enormous private fortunes were made in the plunder, which drove the area to famine in 1768 and 1770. An estimated one-third of the population perished; the company did nothing to intervene. From a moral standpoint, the Bengal famine discredited the East India Company's claim of moral superiority over the "luxurious and despotic Orientals."

In purely practical terms, the company was also shooting itself in the foot. Revenues declined sharply

as the Bengali economy disintegrated. The shortfall was not offset by increasing profits elsewhere in India, and was exacerbated by rising military expenditures. By 1773, the company was in serious difficulties—at which point the British government stepped in. A Regulating Act was passed by parliament, giving London greater control over company affairs, and a governor-general was appointed to supervise Britain's overall interests in India.

The Consolidation of British Control

The first governor-general, serving from 1773 to 1784, was Warren Hastings. By this stage, the Mughal Empire was in a state of open collapse, and Hastings took full advantage of the times. The Marathas cut a swath through the north, capturing Agra and finally Delhi. In support of the kingdom of Awadh (Oudh), Hastings concentrated his forces against the Rohilla, a group of Afghan raiders. He stripped the Nawab of Bengal of his cosmetic powers, and ceased tribute payments to the Mughals. The company's main target was now Haider Ali (1722-1822). Hastings contracted alliances with Awadh, Benares, and other fragments of the former Mughal Empire to oppose him. To finance his campaigns, he turned to extortion. "Allies" paid protection money —or faced British cannons.

In 1784, Hastings returned home to England, where he faced charges of criminal extortion. Writer Edmund Burke led the prosecution, and the trial produced a famous essay as well as victory for Hastings. After proceedings that lasted ten years, however, the ex-governor was a ruined man. Warren Hastings was a contradictory figure, representative of the best and the worst aspects of Britain's pre-Raj presence in India. He was not just a greedy bureaucrat-general;

ABOVE: Everywhere you go in India people are selling their wares. This stall is peddling religious paraphernalia at the roadside—similar stalls just as often sell farm produce or pots and pans.

he was also deeply interested in classical Indian philosophy and religion. Hastings encouraged the first translation of the *Bhagavad Gita* section of the *Mahabharata* into English and wrote the preface to the work.

Company authority continued to grow steadily through the early nineteenth century. By 1845, the Dutch and Austrians had lost their territories. Hastings' successor, Cornwallis, placed the Company's finances on a more stable footing. Territorial expansion was achieved in a series of victorious wars against the Marathas and Mysore. The Anglo-Sikh wars of 1845-1846 and 1848-1849 demonstrated to the entire subcontinent that the new power would tolerate no rivals, even at a regional level. Another means of garnering territory was the Doctrine of Lapse instituted by Lord Dalhousie, under which any Indian state that failed to produce a male heir was annexed.

Increasingly, the British found that they were required to govern and produce social policies as well as simply turning a profit. Social policy required that the British explain to themselves exactly what they were doing in India. The ideology of the Raj—the British Empire in India—began to take shape some decades before the empire itself was proclaimed. Central to this ideology was the idea that the British presence was of benefit to the Indians themselves, and that British rule offered the local populations a chance of access to the rule of law and social progress that they could not hope to achieve through self-government. An early intervention was the banning of suttee—the practice of Hindu widows joining their dead husbands on the funeral pyre—in 1829.

The social reform approach became much more proactive under the governorships of Dalhousie and Canning in the 1840s and 1850s. Indian rulers were liable to be denounced as corrupt, incompetent, or despotic by the governor-general and have their territories seized. A spectacular example was the East India Company's long-time ally, the Nawab of Awadh; the seizure of his principality in 1857 put the company on a path to self-destruction.

The Sepoy Rebellion/India's First War of Independence

On May 10, 1857, a detachment of Muslim troops working for the British and stationed in Meerut, just north of Delhi, was issued with new rifles. The Pattern 1853 Enfield was not a problem; the new rifle's cartridges, greased with animal fats, were: they managed to offend both the Hindus and Muslims simultaneously. The Muslim sepoys marched the 50 miles to Delhi and offered their services to the Mughal Emperor, Bahadur Shah Zafar II. Sporadic fighting broke out all over northern India. Awadh rebelled, as did the Maratha-dominated areas.

By the end of the month, large swaths of the country were back in Indian hands. The rebellion was chaotic; the events in Meerut set a butterfly effect into motion. There was no prior planning or central organization to the uprising. Decades of pent-up frustration and resentment at the company's domination were released in an escalating, perfect storm. The British were entirely unprepared for it when it broke.

Panic and rage fuelled atrocious behavior on both sides as the conflict swirled across the country. In the end, the British prevailed, though at times the outcome seemed in doubt. Most of the sepoys remained on the British side. Delhi was recaptured before the end of the year, and the main concentration of insurgents was overcome in June 1858 at Gwailor in Madhya Pradesh. A remainder made a fighting retreat into Nepal the following year, but the hostilities were essentially finished by mid-1858. So was the East India Company.

Certain Indian historians label the events of 1857-1858 the First War of Indian Independence, pointing out that this was the first concerted push against British domination. While this is certainly true, it is open to question if those who fought and died did so for the sake of an independent India in a sense that modern citizens of the federal republic would recognize. The name given by Britain at the time to the events was as unambiguous as it was insulting: the Great Mutiny. The name is as good an indication as any of why the events took place.

Colonial India

Events moved swiftly following the stabilization of the country. Bahadur Shah Zafar II was arrested for sedition and packed off to exile in Burma (under British control since 1885). The Mughal Empire breathed its last. So did the East India Company, which was dissolved despite an eloquent defense by John Stuart Mill, the commissioner for correspondence at India House in London. India became a Crown Colony under direct British Government control. A Secretary of State for India was added to the cabinet. The office of governor-general was retained in India, and the title of viceroy added for use in his dealings with the remaining Indian princes as a direct representative of the crown. The Doctrine of Lapse was rescinded, and the remaining 562 princes confirmed in their positions. These were a diverse group, including Hindus, Muslims, Sikhs, and others, but were relatively powerless. With only about 40 percent of the national territory and 20 percent of the population in their hands, they were entirely unable to challenge the British rule. The "Native States" rapidly declined into rural backwaters, notable for the splendor of their rulers' uniforms and not much else.

The remaining three-quarters of the population were subject to the administration of the Indian Civil Service. This was a body entirely staffed by a native British workforce, under the control of the governor-general. The provincial governors answered to him, and the district officials answered to them. The system was buttressed by the creation of provincial and legislative councils to formulate and implement policies. The commanding heights in the professions of law and medicine were occupied by an influx from the British Isles.

A colonial society developed that differed in many ways from the old East India Company's world. The merchants had lived side-by-side with the local population, learning the languages and marrying in. They did not recognize any major gap in prestige or technology between the two cultures. Often enough, the British were engaged in all-out war with a relatively equal foe.

The atmosphere was very different in the Raj, as colonial India came to be called. British military power was now completely unassailable, and British society in India grew arrogant, and disdainful of the local populations. Long-standing attitudes of distrust and contempt, which had been present since the "Black Hole of Calcutta" incident, flowered into a full-blown case of the "White Man's Burden." "We felt superior to them [the Indians] in every way," one elderly British lady remarked of her childhood in India during the 1920s—"physically, culturally and morally." Private country clubs catering to an exclusively European clientele sprang up throughout British South Asia, rubbing further salt into the wounds. Decades after independence, their doors remained firmly barred to the local Indian elites. On the other hand, the British left local cultures largely alone. There were no officially sponsored attempts to convert populations to Anglicanism or any other variety of Christianity. English was not forced on the population, though as the language of government and upward social mobility, it spread throughout India on its own.

For a time, *Pax Brittanica*—"British Peace," referring to the relative quiet under imperial rule—descended on the subcontinent. The economy developed, and in 1853 the first railway lines were built, with government encouragement. The population surged upwards. But technological progress did not keep up, especially down on the farm where it counted most. The problem was exacerbated by the administration's fondness for absentee landlords (especially in Bengal and Orissa), and its encouragement of a plantation cash crop economy in many parts of the country. Famine returned to India during the second half of the nineteenth century, striking in Bengal, Tamil Nadu, and Bihar among other provinces. Between 20 and 30 million people died. There were voices of protest in Britain, among them William Digby, but there were others who held that famine relief would merely encourage native laziness. On the whole, too little was done to combat widespread poverty and malnutrition.

The Empire of India

In 1877, Queen Victoria was proclaimed Empress of India in a series of lavish festivities that formed the high-water mark of European imperialism. In her proclamation to the "Princes, Chiefs and Peoples of India," the newly crowned empress pledged to treat all the subjects of the empire impartially under British law. There can be no doubt that she was sincere in her promise, and that the bulk of the general public in Britain shared her sense of idealism. The Indians, of course, saw matters through a different set of lenses. At least, the surviving elites did. The bulk of the population was composed of peasants who were socially powerless and politically illiterate. Things were starting to change, however.

In 1883, the Government of India decided that reform was due in the court system. It introduced measures whereby Indian judges would be empowered to try criminal cases in which Europeans were the accused. The storm of protest that followed in both India and the British press amounted to a "White Mutiny." There were major street demonstrations in Kolkata. The governor-general, George Robinson, soon backed down and amended his proposals. The educated Bengali Hindus looked on with deep interest. British power, it seemed, had its weak points after all.

In 1885, the Indian National Congress was established as a pressure group, with a core group composed of lawyers. This was a decisive step leading the Indian independence movement along a constitutional and non-violent path. The adoption of peaceful reform strategies was not inevitable in India; there were also nationalists at work who preferred violence. Armed revolutionaries carried out a campaign of assassinations against British officials in Bengal, and in Maharashtra the fiery radical Bal Gangadhar Tilak led a similar campaign of violence. But these were also the years in which English-language culture began to sink roots into Indian soil; the growing Indian middle class used the language for business, journalism, political campaigning, and even increasingly in their own families. Partly for this reason, both sides in the emerging struggle were to share enough common ground to keep things remarkably peaceful.

A first step towards greater Indian power was taken in 1892, with the passage of the Indian Councils Act. The viceroy was furnished with Indian advisors, and the appointment of Indian members to provincial and legislative councils. These were very

ABOVE: About seven miles north east of Jaipur lies the Amber Fort. It was originally built in the eleventh century but was greatly extended and improved by Raja Man Singh I in the late 1590s. It gets its name from the goddess Amba Mata—the Mother Earth—who was worshiped here by the local Mina tribe before the fort was built by the Kachhawaha Rajputs. It is one of the most popular visitor destinations in India.

Muslim League, in 1907. Indian Muslims faced a quandary. What was their position to be in a mainly Hindu subcontinent as Indians slowly regained power? The ambivalence of their situation was exploited by the government, which covertly encouraged the growth of the Muslim League as a counterweight to the Swadeshi Movement and the Indian National Congress. But the tide of change was gathering pace.

In 1909, the administration passed the Government of India Act, which was the ultimate forerunner of the Indian Constitution in the post-independence era. Voting rights were extended to a small percentage of the Indian middle class, grouped in separate electorates according to ethnicity and religion. Indians were elected to the national and provincial legislative councils. In the national council, they were heavily outnumbered by government appointees, but they formed a majority in the provincial assemblies. Neither the viceroy nor the provincial governors were answerable to the legislative councils they headed.

The Government of India Act was not intended as a recipe for an independent India, but by the early twentieth century, civil service posts were becoming increasingly occupied by Indians, forming a school of administration for local talent. The Government of India Act effectively set up the provincial councils as a school of governing for Indians. Increasingly, Hindus and Muslims began to see their interests and future as shared. From its own perspective, however, the Raj was in India to stay. A splendid new capital was established at New Delhi, to replace the old one at Kolkata. Designed by the renowned architect Edwin Lutyens, New Delhi expressed the ambitions of British India in stone. When Britain entered World War I in 1914, the viceroy Charles Hardinge, 1st Baron Hardinge of Penshurst, declared India at war with Germany. He saw no need to inform the Indians themselves in advance.

The Road to Independence

The Indian contribution to the imperial war effort was substantial. More than one million Indians saw service overseas, in Europe and (towards the end of the war) in Mesopotamia. Roughly 100,000 of them were killed or wounded. The demands of total war in Europe caused a temporary change in the bizarre pattern of British military recruitment in India—the "Martial Races" theory. This theory was the brainchild of Frederick Sleigh Roberts, Earl of Kandahar, Pretoria and Waterford, a commander-in-chief of Indian forces and a veteran of the Sepoy Rebellion. His experiences convinced him that Punjabis and other north-westerners had an inborn propensity for bravery in war, which was not shared by Bengalis and southerners. The ease of living in hot southern

PAGE 22–23: Huge carved stone elephants guard the entrance to the Jagat Shiromani Temple in the old town of Amber. The temple was built in 1601 in the Rajput style with elaborate Hindu decoration. It was commissioned by Shri Kankawatiji, Maharani of Maharaja Man Singh I in memory of her beloved son Maharaja Kumar Jagat Singhj who had died two years earlier. The temple is home to an idol of Lord Krishna.

limited measures; the viceroy's advisors were powerless, and the council members were hand picked, not elected. It was a classic case of raising a subject population's aspirations just high enough to disappoint them.

Matters reached a head in Bengal in 1905. The government decided that the presidency there had become too large to handle, and proposed partitioning the area into Hindu-dominated West Bengal and Muslim-dominated East Bengal. The move sparked a Hindu-led resistance campaign, the Swadeshi (Boycott) Movement. Significantly, the campaign was non-violent, based on strikes and non-cooperation as well as boycotts of British-made goods. The lessons of the "White Mutiny" of twenty years before had been learned successfully. The government backed down, and the partition was annulled in 1911.

The disappointed Muslim community in Bengal was pushed into forming its own organization, the climes, he argued, sapped their zeal for fighting. His ideas were taken seriously, and from the late nineteenth century until independence (with breaks for the world wars) most Indians were barred from joining the Indian Army.

The outbreak of war brought about the return to India of Mohandas Karamchand Gandhi (1869-1948). One of the great figures of the twentieth century, Gandhi towers over the Indian independence movement and stands alongside figures such as Chandragupta and Ashoka as a prime mover of the country's history. He was an unlikely candidate for glory. Born to a prominent merchant family in Gujarat, he was a poor student and a shy, diffident young man. When studying for the bar in London, he experimented with most of the fashionable alternative ideas of the time—Blavatskyism or Theosophism, vegetarianism, and Tolstoyan anarchism. He read the *Bhagavad Gita* for the first time in his life when English friends urged him to do so. He was a notably unsuccessful lawyer during his brief return to India, and in 1893 he accepted a contract to work in Durban, South Africa.

The naked racism of South African society radicalized Gandhi. He fought proposals to strike Indians off the voters' register in Natal, and organized the Natal Indian Congress in 1894 to channel the struggle. On the outbreak of the Boer War, he argued that Indians should support the British side if they expected to attain full citizenship. He was now an experienced political agitator. His real evolution began after the war's end, in 1906. Launching a protest movement against anti-Indian discrimination in the Transvaal, he expounded the principle of *satyagraha* (devotion to the truth) as the basis of a mass non-violent movement of passive resistance. He was now starting to reach deep into India's past, drawing on its traditions as a personal source of moral strength. The further he reached, the stronger he became. Despite beatings, arrests, and imprisonments, the Transvaal campaign succeeded. On his return to India, Gandhi abandoned Western-style clothes in favor of a simple dhoti robe, or often just a loincloth, as worn by India's poorest people. Alexander's Greeks had been awed by the mental balance and determination of the gymnosophists, or naked philosophers; here was a signal that the British were to face a gymnosophist of their own. They were to prove woefully unequal as intellectual rivals.

The burgeoning independence movement was still in a fluid state, and the pressures of war moved Hindu and Muslim activists towards closer alliances. The Congress Party (as the Indian National Congress had become known) held joint sessions with the Muslim League in late 1916 under the leadership of Motilal Nehru, father of Jawaharlal Nehru, and Muhammad Ali Jinnah. The deal hammered out was satisfactory to both sides. Congress accepted the League's policy of separate electorates, and the League agreed to campaign for self-government. The Raj responded to the increased pressure by promising increased political authority for Indians. The promise bore fruit in the Government of India Act of 1919, which substantially increased voting rights and extended Indian power at the provincial level. There were strict limits to these concessions, however. In the regions, British officials still held the reins in financial and policing affairs, and at the top the viceroy remained solely answerable to the British government.

World War I caused great anxiety for Muslims, because among Britain's enemies was the Ottoman Empire, the world's only Islamic power at that time. The advance into Mesopotamia raised a storm of protest, which the Turkish surrender did nothing to abate. There were fears—well founded, as it turned out—that the office of the Caliph would be abolished. The Caliph, based in Istanbul, was the spiritual head of Sunni Islam, and a focus of Muslim loyalty after the fall of the Mughal Empire. Starting in 1917, the Khalifat Movement, which arose to protest the Allies' plans, won over whole new sections of Muslim popular opinion to support for a self-governing India.

World War I opened up a window of political opportunity in India; but predictably enough, when the war ended the shutters came back down. Opposition newspapers were censored, opposition leaders were jailed, and marches and demonstrations were banned. Congress held mass protests across the country, organized on the non-violent principles of Gandhi, who was now starting to come to the forefront. Not all of these protests remained nonviolent. Martial law was declared in areas where British authority was deemed insecure. One such area was the Punjab, under the governorship of Sir Michael O'Dwyer. On April 13, 1919, thousands of people gathered in Amritsar for the Sikh religious festival of Baisakhi. The assembly was in contravention of martial law. The local British and Gurkha forces under General Reginald Dyer reacted with ferocity. An assault took place on the crowds gathered in a walled park in the city, and somewhere between 379 and 2,000 civilians lost their lives. The damage to British moral authority was even greater.

Gandhi became the leading figure in the reaction that followed. He was elected president of the All-India Home Rule League in 1920, and became the leader of the Congress Party in 1921. Gandhi transformed Congress into an organized mass movement with independence as its stated goal. He urged an expanded policy of non-cooperation with British rule. The boycott went far beyond British-made goods. British courts and education, honors and

titles, and employment in the civil service all came under fire. He also made his famous appeal for Indians to weave their own cloth as a commitment to economic self-sufficiency. With the question of the Caliphate still hanging in the balance, he tried to keep the Hindu and Muslim movements united by declaring Congress support for the Khalifat Movement.

This first postwar push galvanized India, but ended without success. The Turks, under Kemal Ataturk, decided to abolish the office of Caliph themselves in favor of a secular state. Gandhi decided that the mass campaign of non-cooperation was in danger of degenerating into a turbulence of violent resistance and called off the campaign in early 1922. The authorities, for their part, decided that now was the time to put Gandhi behind bars, and arrested him for sedition in March of the same year. And most discouragingly of all, Hindu-Muslim unity became strained as the euphoria of united action wore off and gave way to a more sober, even fearful, appraisal of each community's conflicting interests.

The Muslim leadership tentatively moved towards the position that Islamic India might require its own state in some form. Jinnah declared in 1921 that "Muslims and Hindus are two major nations by any definition or test of a nation" and that "the true welfare not only of the Muslims but of the rest of India lies in the division of India."

Throughout the remainder of the 1920s, India displayed a kind of quiet and sullen stability. Expectations were focused on the ten-year review of the 1919 Government of India Act, and the gains it might bring. Gandhi, when not in prison, spent his time out of the public eye. However, in 1927 the British government announced a constitutional reform commission in advance of the ten-year review; not a single Indian was named to it. Gandhi now launched a Congress campaign calling for Dominion status for India within a year. (A Dominion was a self-governing member of the British Empire—for example, Canada.) When no government answer was forthcoming, Gandhi launched one of his most famous acts of civil resistance, the Salt March of 1930. Leading an ever-growing host of followers, he marched 248 miles from Ahmedabad to the coast at Dandi, and made salt in defiance of a government monopoly. More than 60,000 people were arrested in the campaign. By 1931, his implacable will had worn down the government. The Gandhi-Irwin Pact was signed, under which the political prisoners were set free in exchange for an end to civil disobedience—after which the cycle of government repression began all over again.

On the constitutional front, limited reforms continued. A series of conferences that Gandhi attended in London through the early 1930s yielded the Government of India Act of 1935. Real progress towards self-government was made at the provincial level. Elected Indian politicians now took control of finances and taxation. Fewer concessions were given in New Delhi; the crucial areas of government remained in British hands. A particular point of conflict was Britain's continued support of separate communal electorates. Congress by this stage had reversed its earlier policy and called for unified elections. This drove a further wedge between Congress and the League. Moreover, the remaining Indian princes were highly reluctant to see any measure of democracy introduced into their domains. The Raj obliged them by not extending the 1935 reforms to the states under their control.

With this unsatisfactory level of reform in place, India settled back down to a relative calm. The Congress and Muslim League politicians tested the limits of their new powers. Jawaharlal Nehru became the Congress Party leader. Gandhi, rather disenchanted with politics, campaigned on behalf of India's lowest castes—the so-called "Untouchables." He gave them a new name: the Harijans, or "Children of God."

World War II and the End of the British Empire in India

For Indians, World War II started in exactly the same way as World War I. With no prior consultation, the viceroy—Victor Alexander John Hope, Marquis of Linlithgow—declared the country to be at war with Germany on September 3, 1939. Recruitment was thrown open to all races "martial" and "non-martial," and by war's end the Indian Army numbered more than two million. It was the largest volunteer force ever assembled in history. Indian troops fought in Burma and Southeast Asia, the Middle East, Africa, and Italy.

Gandhi had supported the British Empire in its various conflicts since the Boer War, in the hope that loyalty would be rewarded with political progress. This time was different. He and Congress declared that the victims of fascist aggression had their full sympathy, but that India could no longer be expected to fight for democratic freedoms abroad while those very freedoms continued to be denied at home. Independence could not wait. His campaign slogan was now completely uncompromising: "Quit India."

Mass protests occurred on a scale never witnessed before, and there were widespread outbreaks of violence. Communal solidarity was strained. In 1940,

RIGHT: Colorful saris stand out from the mud floor. Indian textiles are often brighter than one would expect.

INDIRA GHANDI

Indira Nehru Gandhi (1917-1984) was born on November 19, 1917, the only child of Jawaharlal Nehru, whose role as leader of India she later assumed. She became politically active at the age of 12 as the leader of the Monkey Brigade, a group of children dedicated to the removal of the British rule in India. In 1938 Indira joined the National Congress Party and in 1942 she married the journalist Feroze Gandhi. They were both sent to prison by the British for subversion; Indira was sent to the Naini Central Jail in Allahabad on September 11, 1942, until May 13, 1943. When India became independent from Britain in 1947 her father became prime minister. Indira acted as official hostess and aide for the widowed Nehru, and in the process met many influential world political figures. She used the knowledge and contacts she gained to become only the fourth woman elected to the Indian National Congress in 1955; she became president of the body in 1959. On her father's death in 1964 the new prime minister, Lal Bahadur Shastri, appointed Indira Minister of Information and Broadcasting. Shastri died in 1966 and Indira was made the temporary, compromise prime minister until being elected in her own right in 1967. In her attempts to modernize India she made many enemies. Inflation rose, the economy was in ruins, and corruption endemic. In 1975 Indira was charged with using illegal campaign practices. In response, she refused to resign and instead declared a state of emergency, censored the press, and ordered the arrest of her chief political opponents. She had become dictator of India. In 1977 she allowed free elections and was voted out of office. Indira became prime minister again in 1980. After ordering the storming of the Sikh Golden Temple in Amritsar she was assassinated at home by her Sikh bodyguards on October 31, 1984.

the Muslim league formally called for the creation of a separate Pakistani state. Religious riots increased sharply, and the authorities did little or nothing to stop them. Even Gandhi's pacifism seemed to be wearing thin after decades of political obstruction. Real anarchy, he publicly mused in 1942, could hardly be any worse than the "ordered anarchy" of wartime British India. He was promptly arrested and imprisoned.

The Allied collapse in Europe and Southeast Asia led other nationalists to even more extreme conclusions. Subhas Chandra Bose had been a fiery supporter of armed struggle even when he was a leading light of the Congress Party. After he left it in 1937, he set up his own organization, which leaned towards the expanding power of Japan. Japan had been an inspiration for Asian nationalists ever since it defeated Russia in 1904-1905. Now the Japanese were threatening every European colony in East Asia, and calling for the creation of a "Co-Prosperity Sphere" under the slogan "Asia for the Asians." It was intoxicating propaganda. By 1940, Bose was in Tokyo.

There were 60,000 Indian troops among the men captured when the Japanese stormed Singapore in 1942. From among them and other Indian communities in Southeast Asia, Bose recruited a small army of 25,000. The group was styled the Azad Hind Fauj, or Free India Army. It posed no real threat to British India. A few thousand FIA troops saw action in the Japanese offensive in Burma in 1944. But the Japanese never afforded Bose any genuine measure of decision-making power, and as their empire disintegrated under a hail of American bombs, so did the Indian National Army. Bose himself is thought to have died in a plane crash while fleeing to Taiwan in the closing days of the war. Viewed through Indian eyes, he is a complex, even tragic figure. All that can be stated certainly of the whole affair is that if Bose had not allied himself with the Japanese, some other Indian leader would have. His mistake was to think that a Japanese-dominated India could have been freer than a British-dominated one.

British domination itself plainly became more and more untenable as the war progressed. The resources no longer existed to maintain an empire on the grand scale, and the home country came to depend militarily and economically on the United States. Churchill grumbled that he had not been elected "to preside over the dissolution of the British Empire." It was left to his successor Clement Atlee to bow to the inevitable and declare in 1946 that Britain would grant independence to India. The question was partition. Although Congress and the British were reluctant to accept the idea, the logic of the situation forced their hand. The likelihood was that a united independent India would have immediately

descended into civil war. A Direct Action Day organized by the Muslim League saw massive bloodshed in Kolkata. The partition of the Indus Valley and East Bengal from the remainder of India was decided at a meeting between Jinnah and the last Viceroy Lord Louis Mountbatten on June 3, 1947. On August 15, the self-governing dominions of India and Pakistan were created.

There was an immediate and catastrophic exodus of Muslims into Pakistan and Hindus into India. More than ten million people fled on horrific journeys through hostile populations. Perhaps half a million died on the way. Desperate border conflicts immediately broke out between the two Dominions, with especially intense fighting in Kashmir, a

Muslim-majority principality whose Hindu prince had decided to stay with India. Fighting continued until January 1949, with about 1,500 casualties on both sides. Many thousands more were to perish in sporadic fighting over the coming decades. The year 1948 saw the deaths of the titanic figures who had led the drive to independence. Gandhi was heartbroken by the partition of India, which he regarded as a mutilation of his country. At times during his final two years he went on hunger strike, attempting to halt inter-communal violence. He was assassinated on January 30 by a Hindu extremist. Mohammed Ali Jinnah passed away from tuberculosis on September 11 in Karachi, the city he had personally chosen as the capital of the state he had created.

The Federal Republic of India

The final link with Britain was severed when India adopted a republican constitution on January 26, 1950. Pakistan in turn adopted an Islamic Constitution. Jawaharlal Nehru took his place at the helm of the world's largest democratic state. It held out much promise, and was beset with many problems. One of the promises of the new state was enshrined in the declaration: *The institution of caste is abolished and its practice is outlawed.* The problems included continued caste discrimination, inter-communal tension, and above all, poverty.

In the 1950s, the Soviet Union was the great model of a state lifting itself by the bootstraps from

ABOVE: Virupaksha Temple, Hampi, northern Karnataka is dedicated to Shiva and is still in use. The 160ft high gopuram dates from the sixteenth century. Surrounding it are the ruins of the city of Vijayanagara, the capital of the Vijayanagara Empire which lasted from 1336 until 1565. The entire area is a World Heritage site.

poverty to industrial and political might. Nehru had been to Moscow and seen for himself, and decided that "the human costs are unpayable." Five-year plans for economic growth were adopted, but state ownership of enterprise was restricted to a few key industries. The Soviet Union provided some aid and technological assistance to balance the United States' support of Pakistan, but the Indian economy remained chronically undercapitalized until the dawn of the "dotcom" era. State control of big business was complemented by crony capitalism in the small business sector; for business people to cut through thick layers of red tape, close and profitable relationships with local politicians and bureaucrats proved necessary.

Despite its many problems, India made great achievements in its early post-colonial years. The Federal Republic proved to be a stable political framework on which to build a working democracy. It could very easily have turned out to be a different and bloodier enterprise. The political, judicial, and educational systems were inherited from the empire, and Britain prides itself with some justification that they were handed over intact and in working order. For contrast, one can point to many empires that ransacked and abandoned their colonies to civil war and dictatorship. Nevertheless, the colonial legacy warped Indian democracy in subtle ways. The Indian Parliament convened in a spanking new building in New Delhi—but the number of deputies in the elected Lok Sabha was the same as the House of Commons in London. The judiciary, police and local governments inherited the mindset of their former masters, and saw their role as controlling the population rather than carrying out its will. Along with corruption, this inherent democratic deficit has been an endemic problem in the functioning of the state.

By disposition, Nehru was a pacifist, but he was prepared to use force in reclaiming Hyderabad in 1948, where the situation was the reverse of Kashmir —the local Muslim prince ruled over a majority Hindu state. In 1961, the Indian army took Goa in a bloodless strike, after repeated requests to the Portuguese to return the area had fallen on deaf ears.

India's first defeat came the following year. The Chinese People's Liberation Army attacked Arunachal Pradesh and Ladakh. The Chinese had fielded their strongest army in centuries against the Americans in Korea, and with the memory still fresh they were spoiling to recover disputed territories in India. They largely succeeded. The Indian Army was poorly trained and under-equipped. Nehru was unprepared for the assault—he saw China as a partner in the global Non-Aligned Movement, which India headed. The defeat cast a shadow of the remaining years of his premiership. He passed away in 1964.

Indira Gandhi

Nehru's daughter Indira Gandhi (no relation to Mohandas) took over running the country in 1966, after the brief prime ministership of Congress politician Lal Bahadur Shastri. As a female leader in a deeply patriarchal society, she was at first derided by many as a "dumb doll" and dismissed as a puppet. Her critics were profoundly mistaken. She was a consummate politician, and power-hungry to the point where she almost turned India into a dictatorship. She first surrounded herself with a cabinet of sycophants, and spent time entrenching her supporters in the upper echelons of the government and administration. The Congress Party itself proved an obstacle; she set up a party of her own in 1969.

On winning the 1971 election, she launched the army into another war. Pakistan was breaking up. Its Eastern and Western components were separated by hundreds of miles, and they were linguistically and culturally quite distinct in everything but Islam. The Bengalis resented the West Pakistanis' iron grip on power, and began a separatist campaign for an independent Bangladesh. They were desperate when India intervened. Millions of terrorized civilians fled the Pakistani Army's campaign by crossing the border into India. The military strikes ordered by Indira Gandhi quickly tipped the scales in the insurgents' favor. Bangladesh was created in the teeth of U.S. opposition, but Gandhi held her line in this classic Cold War showdown. The Soviet Union had promised to intervene if Nixon entered the conflict directly.

As Prime Minister, Indira Gandhi was as resourceful as she was belligerent. A major legacy of her period in office was the Green Revolution, a science-spurred change in farming that raised crop yields, in turn lifting hundreds of millions out of poverty. She also made India a nuclear energy producer, and laid the groundwork for the country's nuclear weapons program. Trouble brewed in the miniature Himalayan protectorate of Sikkim. Gandhi annexed it. When the High Court convicted her of electoral fraud in 1975, she immediately suspended the constitution and commenced a draconian regime of government by decree. The discipline she imposed was welcome to some, but the price was not far from fascism. The press was censored, opposition leaders were jailed, and thousands of women were forcibly sterilized in a ham-handed attempt to emulate China's population control policies. Gandhi's son Sanjay was being groomed as her successor; he was an active supporter of his mother's unsavory tactics.

Absolved of fraud in 1977, Gandhi presented herself to a grateful populace for reelection, and was soundly defeated. She grudgingly handed power to the opposition Janata Coalition, led by Morarji Desai.

LEFT: City Palace, Jaipur, Rajasthan. The palace is a sprawling collection of buildings and courtyard gardens, terraces, pathways, and fountains. It includes the Chandra Mahal (or Moon Palace), Mubarak Mahal, Badal Mahal, Shri Govind Dev Temple, and the City Palace Museum.

Gandhi's second term of office lasted from 1980 until her assassination in 1984. It was marred by the death of Sanjay Gandhi in a dubious plane crash, and the crisis at the Golden Temple in Amritsar. Sikh political aspirations had been radicalized under the influence of the militant religious leader Sant Jarnail Singh Bhindranwale, who declared the Punjab a sovereign Sikh state. A Pakistani-supported insurgent campaign culminated in the seizure of the Golden Temple by militants in June 1984. Gandhi reflexively sent in the troops. The resulting bloodbath killed more than 500 defenders and attackers, and enraged the entire Sikh community. This included Gandhi's trusted bodyguards, who turned their guns on her on October 31. Anti-Sikh riots left another 3,000 dead in New Delhi.

Contemporary India

The main themes in India over the last two decades have been the rise of Hindu nationalism in the shape of the Bharativa Janata Party (the BJP) and the opening up of the economy to foreign investment.

Economic reform was started by Rajiv Gandhi, who succeeded his mother and was himself assassinated in 1991, probably by a Sri Lankan Tamil Tiger. His successor, P.V. Rao, opened up the economy further, kick-starting the remarkable growth of the "back office" business, which provides international clerical and technical services via telephone and the Internet. This new sector has bolstered the traditionally underemployed Indian middle class and boosted its spending power. The social and economic effects of the new economy are only starting to make themselves felt, and they are changing the face of India. It is now the world's tenth-largest economy and still growing.

P.V. Rao's Congress Party lost to the BJP in 1996. The Hindu nationalist party prospered on the stresses and discontents of rapid social change, and offered the nation a new-style aggressive traditionalism as the cure. However, two chaotic years of short-lived multi-party governments followed before the BJP finally returned to power. Prime Minister Atal Bihari Vajpayee led a turbulent and controversial administration between March 1998 and May 2004.

India became a nuclear-armed state in May 1998, drawing international condemnation. Pakistan already possessed nuclear weapons. Between April and June 1999, armed confrontation broke out again in Kashmir. All-out war was barely averted. Relations have improved under the Congress government of Manmohan Singh, India's first Sikh Prime Minister, who took office in May 2004. The Congress Party is led by Sonya Gandhi, the widow of Rajiv Gandhi. The tsunami of December 2004 caused major damage to India's east coast, and killed an estimated 16,413 people. Unexpected though the setback was, it has not halted India's progress towards ever-increasing regional influence and economic prosperity.

India and the World

India's main historic impact on the outside world has been cultural. Much in the same way that the Roman Empire influenced Europe, Indian models of culture, governance, religion, and literacy set important precedents and standards in Sri Lanka and Southeast Asia. Continental Southeast Asia has retained a distinctive mix of Buddhist religion and architecture, and alphabetic scripts derived from Brahmic. Malaysia and the Indonesian archipelago adopted the Roman alphabet from the British and Dutch, respectively. But here, too, Hinduism and Islam—as transmitted from India—form the backbone of the cultures. Further afield, in China, Korea, and Japan, Indian influences were assimilated into already

BELOW: One of a number of ornate carved alabaster lattice windows in the Amber Fort, Jaipur. These screens were set at ground level so that in the stifling heat of summer even the slightest breeze would be caught.

existing complex historical cultures with varying degrees of success. Buddhism has survived in all three countries in harmony (and sometimes competition) with Taoism, Confucianism, and Shinto.

Sri Lanka adopted Buddhism early, around 240 B.C., and the Tripitaka canon of Theravada Buddhism was written in the Pali alphabet. From there, the religion and alphabet spread into Southeast Asia. The movement was peaceful. The foundation myth of Cambodia tells of a Brahmin priest called Kaundinya, who appeared "from the sea" as a dragon-lord, and won the hand of the local dragon-princess. The dragon-lord then drank up the water that covered the land, established a capital and named the new country "Kambuja." The Khmer *devaraja* (god-kings) adopted Indian names and culture, and built a mighty capital at Angkor from the early tenth century.

Indian influence spread beyond Cambodia into Champa, in what is now the south of Vietnam. In Sumatra, the kingdom of Srivjaya acted as a cultural conduit into Java, Bali, and Lombok. Today, Bali retains a vibrant Hindu culture that it has made its very own. Myanmar was heavily influenced by India from its inception, and the first major capital—

Pagan, built in A.D. 842—is a masterpiece of Buddhist architecture.

The northern route of Buddhist missionary activity brought Indian influence into Tibet and China. Mahayana Buddhism recognized local deities as bodhisattvas (incarnations of the Buddha) or as Buddhist saints under a different aspect, thus helping its spread. Esoteric Tantric Buddhism developed a tradition of secret transmission under guru-like teachers, which appealed to Taoists and helped in the development of Chan (or, in Japan, Zen) Buddhism.

Chinese Buddhist communities flourished in the capital Loyang from about A.D. 150, and monasticism spread throughout the country. By the fourth century, however, Confucianism had become the dominant state ideology. Confucianism had major problems with the Buddhist monastic ideal, because of the conflict between the demands of the meditative life and respectful piety. Buddhism was discouraged in China from the eighth century and in Korea from the fifteenth century in favor of Confucianism.

In Japan, Buddhism became the state religion in the sixth century, and the Shinto gods were accepted as Buddhist saints. A major Buddhist culture developed in Kyoto, a city with more than a thousand temples.

ABOVE: Jantar Mantar (The Observatory), in Jaipur. This was the second of five observatories built by Raja Sawai Jai Singh II and attracted scholars and scientists from all over India and Europe who marveled at its facilities. Among other things it can mark time to the accuracy of a second. The Rajah was a considerable astronomical scholar himself, and before embarking on building work for his observatories sent his emissaries out far and wide to collect the very latest astronomical instruments from around the world.

Despite persecution in the late 1500s (the monks had become too powerful), Buddhism has thrived in Japan more than in any other East Asian country. Vast swaths of the culture from tea ceremony to martial arts are informed by Buddhist ideas of "no-self" directly stemming from India's Ganga Valley.

The eastward spread of Hinduism, Buddhism, and Islam from India involved relatively few people actually leaving the subcontinent. The British Raj changed all that. In the 1800s, thousands of Indian traveled to distant parts of the British Empire as indentured laborers—to South Africa, the Caribbean, Guyana, Surinam, Fiji, and Sri Lanka. Traders were especially active in British East Africa, and many Indian soldiers settled down in Africa in the aftermath of various colonial wars. The post-independence diaspora was equally varied. Large numbers of men went to the oil-rich states of the Middle East to work as laborers. Indian labor was especially required in the postwar rebuilding of Britain and the Netherlands, and Britain built up a large community of Indians working in the catering and other trades. These immigrant families have produced a cadre of professionals in medicine, law, and other fields. North America, Canada, and Australia are home to vibrant new Indian communities. The old overseas communities in Malaysia, Singapore, and Hong Kong continue to play a vital role in their respective countries.

The Indian diaspora has given the world an exciting group of modern writers in English. It also exerts a delicate influence on the home country. Support for the BJP style of Hindu nationalism has been evident especially in middle-class communities in the West. The political fallout from Indian emigration has been severest in the island nations of Sri Lanka and Fiji. Sri Lanka is home to a large community of Tamils, brought over to the north and east of the island as cheap labor during the nineteenth century. From the 1980s, the Tamil Tigers have waged a ferocious campaign to create a self-governing state, drawing equally ferocious government countermeasures. Tens of thousands have been killed in the struggle, which saw the first widespread use of suicide bombers as a military tactic. In Fiji, so many Indians were brought to the island as indentured labor that the indigenous Polynesians became a small minority. Feeling that their culture was under threat, the Polynesian-dominated army launched a coup in 2000. Indians have also faced persistent harassment in East Africa, the most notorious case being Idi Amin's wholesale expulsion of the Ugandan Indian community. Despite racism, discrimination, and political problems, the Indian diaspora continues to grow and prosper, bound together above all by shared roots—and Bollywood movies. Bollywood is the latest Indian cultural export, with a wide viewership in the Islamic world as well as in Indian communities across the globe.

Modern Indian Culture

With its vast scale geographical scale and colossal cultural heritage, it's not surprising that India's outstanding single characteristic is its diversity. Unusually for a postcolonial nation, its ancient heritage remains substantially intact. Empires have come and gone, adding layer after layer to the mix, but the age-old realities of village life and religious faith have

changed relatively little in most rural areas. The cities, of course, are a different matter. Gigantic conurbations like Kolkata (population: 15 million) and Mumbai (over 12 million) are at the cutting edge of change in South Asia, and home to large English-speaking, mass-consuming, middle-class communities. Cities like Bangalore are economically hardwired into the global economy through Internet business. A new, youthful generation is overtaking their parents in earning and spending power. Yet even in the large cities, post-modernity is simply often another layer on top of an underlying and largely unchanging basic culture.

But change has been swift enough to create a hunger for the old ways, and globalization has produced losers as well as winners. The traditional culture has come under the kind of paradoxical stresses peculiar to the age of the Internet. The BJP prospered on a strident, sometimes intolerant, platform of militant Hinduism; in various ways, many Indians have turned in recent years towards the certainties offered by religion, caste, and locality.

One flashpoint has been the town of Ayodhya, where a mosque stood on the traditional site of the birthplace of Rama. And caste remains a social reality, no matter what the law may say. Attempts to end the informal quota system of university places for "higher" caste applicants have caused serious student riots. International relief efforts after the 2004 tsunami were dogged by an unwillingness to share emergency accommodation and supplies with the low-status Dalit caste. In some cases, separate camps had to be constructed to allow the relief operations to proceed smoothly. And corruption remains a factor in everyday life, as a recent scandal in which senior government officials were secretly videotaped taking bribes attests.

Despite these concerns, the vibrant energy of the modern Indian street is undeniable. The Bollywood movie is its true mirror—warmhearted, sentimental, colorful, and often completely over the top. Sam Goldwyn famously advised Hollywood filmmakers to "Start with a volcano and then work your way up to a climax." This is where a low-budget Bollywood movie would start; well-funded productions are a good deal more ambitious and spectacular.

As of 2005, India had a population of one billion, and was poised to overtake China as the world's most populous state. The religious makeup of this population breaks down at 80 percent Hindu, 14 percent Muslim, 2.4 percent Christian, 2 percent Sikh, and 1.6 percent Buddhist, Jain, and other. Seventy-two percent of the people speak Indo-European languages, 25 percent Dravidian and 3 percent other languages. As mentioned previously, India is the world's tenth largest economic power, but when purchasing power is taken into account, it emerges as fourth. With an economy growing at more than 5 percent per year, millions are being lifted out of poverty, and the Indian middle class is emerging as a key group of consumers; international corporations are quickly learning to cater to their tastes.

The growing international weight the country enjoys is reflected in its campaign (along with Brazil, Germany, and Japan) for permanent member status of the United Nations Security Council.

BELOW: The best way to enjoy watching wildlife is from the back of an elephant. These tourists are riding through Kaziranga National Park in the Northeastern Hill States, the last place in the world to see *Rhinoceros unicornis*, the rare Indian one-horned rhino.

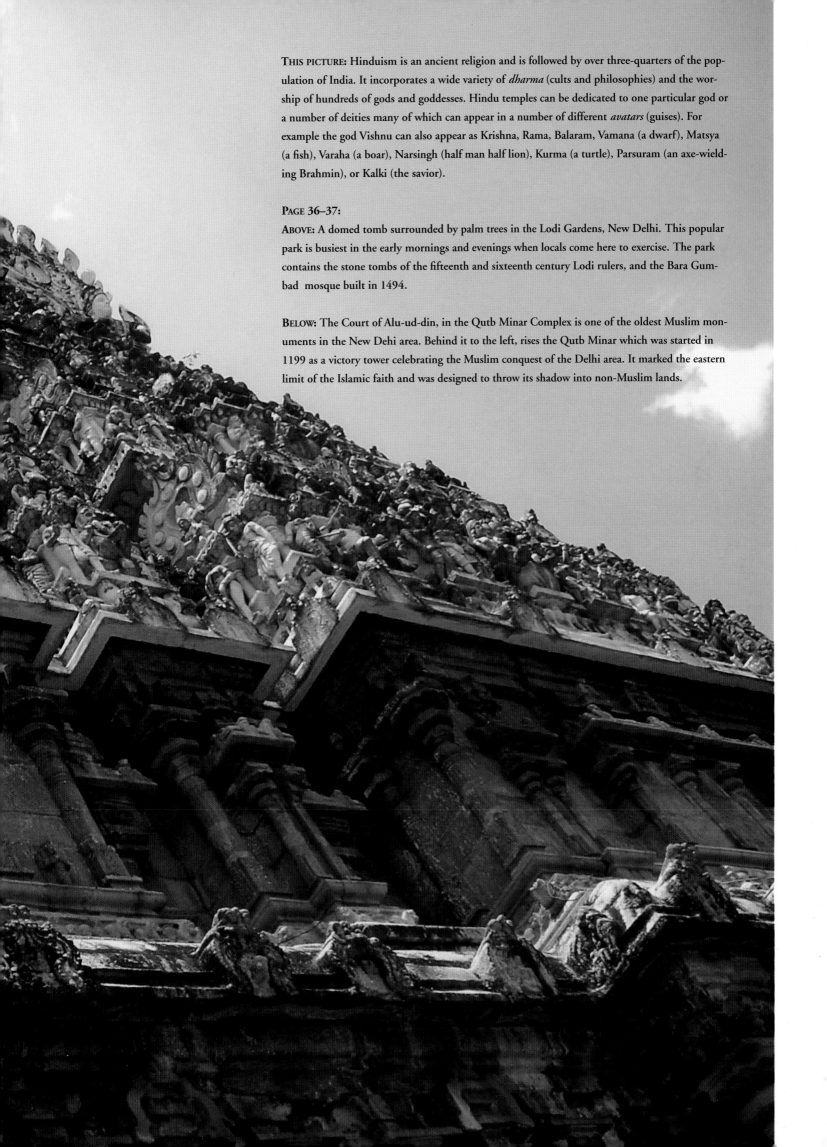

THIS PICTURE: Hinduism is an ancient religion and is followed by over three-quarters of the population of India. It incorporates a wide variety of *dharma* (cults and philosophies) and the worship of hundreds of gods and goddesses. Hindu temples can be dedicated to one particular god or a number of deities many of which can appear in a number of different *avatars* (guises). For example the god Vishnu can also appear as Krishna, Rama, Balaram, Vamana (a dwarf), Matsya (a fish), Varaha (a boar), Narsingh (half man half lion), Kurma (a turtle), Parsuram (an axe-wielding Brahmin), or Kalki (the savior).

PAGE 36–37:

ABOVE: A domed tomb surrounded by palm trees in the Lodi Gardens, New Delhi. This popular park is busiest in the early mornings and evenings when locals come here to exercise. The park contains the stone tombs of the fifteenth and sixteenth century Lodi rulers, and the Bara Gumbad mosque built in 1494.

BELOW: The Court of Alu-ud-din, in the Qutb Minar Complex is one of the oldest Muslim monuments in the New Dehi area. Behind it to the left, rises the Qutb Minar which was started in 1199 as a victory tower celebrating the Muslim conquest of the Delhi area. It marked the eastern limit of the Islamic faith and was designed to throw its shadow into non-Muslim lands.

ABOVE: The Delhi Gate was designed by Edwin Lutyens and built as a memorial to the 70,000 Indian soldiers who died during World War 1. Work started on the red Bharatpur stone landmark in 1921; the monument was dedicated 10 years later. An additional 13,516 names are engraved on the arch and foundations to form a separate memorial to the British and Indian soldiers killed in 1919 on the North-West Frontier during the Afghan War.

RIGHT: At 239ft Qutab Minar at Aurabindo Marg, near Mehrauli, is the tallest stone tower in India and dominates the countryside. Its foundations were laid in 1199 after the victory of Muhammad of Ghur (for Islam) over Prithviraj Chauhan, the last Hindu king of Delhi, in 1192. Qutab Minar was built in three stages which were not completed until 1370. The first three stories are made of red sandstone but levels four and five incorporate marble as well.

LEFT AND BELOW (DETAIL): Lal Quila—better known in the West as the Red Fort—in Delhi was constructed between 1638 and 1648 by Shah Jehan as part of his new capital city, Shahjahanabad which replaced the former capital at Agra. Originally built alongside the Jumna River—which has changed its course since—the waters fed the moats which surrounded the base of most of the walls.

RIGHT: Every market in every city, town, and village across India offers a selection of aromatic herbs and spices which Indians use for medicinal purposes as well as extensively in their cooking.

LEFT: Detail of columnar capital of the temple in Happy Valley Tibetan Refugee Center, painted in traditional Tibetan decoration.

ABOVE: Sunrise over mountains at Dharamsala, where the Dalai Lama and his court live in self-imposed exile from Tibet.

ABOVE: The Jal Mahal Palace in the Nahargarth hills of Rajasthan dates back to the eighteenth century when it was built as a pleasure palace for royal duck-shooting parties. Built alongside the Amber Fort road from Jaipur it is surrounded by the man-made Lake Mansagar. The palace is now abandoned—the lower four floors are under the lake.

RIGHT: Bags of medicinal herbs set out for sale. Aromatic herbs and spices have a long and respected role in Buddhist medicine.

PAGES 44–45: A mountian village in Ladakh, high in the Himalayas. India's most remote and sparsely populated area, it is separated from China and Pakistan by the Himalaya and Karakoram ranges respectively.

PAGE 46–47: The irrigated wheat and barley fields of the Indus Valley contrast with the arid foothills in Thikse, Ladakh. Other crops that can be grown here include apricots, walnuts, and a number of different vegetables.

LEFT: A small boat and a *shikara*—water taxi—cross Nagin Lake at sunset in Kashmir. The lake is famous for its beautiful waterlilies, and exotic houseboats which are popular with visitors, and theshikaras which also work as floating shops.

RIGHT: A river snakes down a valley between Ladakh and Kashmir.

BELOW: Prayer flags leading up to Namgya Tsemo Gompa (Red Gompa) just north of the city of Leh in the Himalayas of Jammu-Kashmir State. The monastery contains a huge statue of Buddha.

PAGE 50–51: Shey Palace was built as the summer palace of the kings. Unfortunately it is now in ruins.

PAGE 52–53: The Golden Temple in Amritsar, Punjab is the spiritual center for Sikhs. The Hari Mandir, the actual golden temple in the Golden Temple complex, sits in the middle of a rectangular sacred pool connected to the rest of the complex by the narrow Guru's Bridge. The temple was built by Guru Arjun (1581–1606) who also compiled the Adi Granth sacred scriptures. The temple was completed in 1601.

LEFT: Amber Fort lies seven miles northeast of Jaipur in the midst of the wild Aravalli hills. It is named after the goddess Amba Mata, who the Mina tribe worshipped here as the Mother Earth. The complex was started in the eleventh century but was considerably improved and extended by Raja Man Singh I (1590–1614) when it was developed as a pleasure palace. The palace stands above Maota Lake which provided the main water supply for the palace. The pleasure chambers were built so that fresh air from the surrounding hills are collected and then cooled over channels of perfumed water before being circulated around the rooms.

LEFT: Detail of a carved ceiling corbel from the Amber Fort. The fort and palace are covered with elaborate decorations.

RIGHT: Deep into the desert lies Jaisalmer, a dramatic fortress city near Pakistan, built in the 1100s. These sculptures of Jain deities are from the temple of Parsvanatha in Jaisalmer.

BELOW: Another view of the Amber Fort.

PAGE 58–59: Jaisalmer Fort is built on top of Trikuta Hill and dominates the desert landscape for miles around. Its massive sandstone walls have stood for over 800 years and are reinforced by 99 massive bastions.

LEFT: Four miles north of Jaipur and just below Nahargarh Fort lie the royal cenotaphs of the Kachhawaha rulers at Gaitor. The biggest and best belongs to Raja Sawai Jai Singh II who died in 1743 at the age of 55.

FAR LEFT AND BELOW: Mehrangarh Fort, Jodhpur sits on top of a 400ft escarpment above the surrounding plains. Some parts of the ramparts are cut from the rock face itself. The fort can only be entered through a zigzag path that runs through a series of fortified gateways.

PAGE 62–63: The waters of Gadisar Lake reflect waterfront temples and shrines. This artificial lake was built by Maharaja Gadsi Singh to store the water supply for Jaisalmer, the golden desert city of Rajasthan.

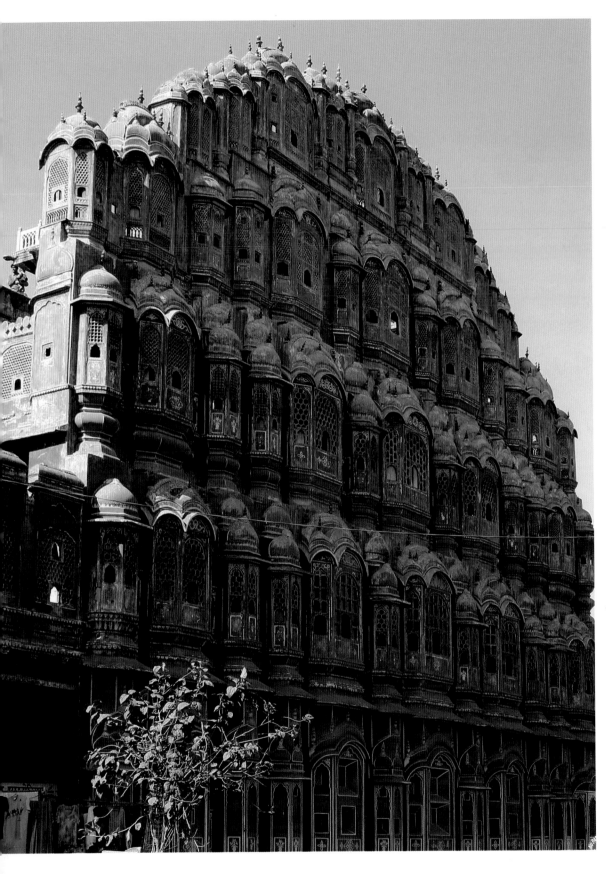

ABOVE AND RIGHT: The Hawa Mahal in Jaipur was built out of red and pink sandstone as part of the City Palace complex by Maharaja Sawai Pratap Singh in 1799. Designed by Lal Chand Usta, at the base are two courtyards above which on the eastern side are three stories only one room deep. The building was part of the womens' quarters and constructed so the ladies of the court could watch goings-on in the street without being seen behind the elegantly and elaborately carved façade. So, in fact, the Hawa Mahal is little more than a privacy screen on a truely magnificent scale. The frontage contains 953 small window niches for the intimate chambers, each of which has its own carved lattice grill and a tiny balcony. The windows are designed to catch even the slightest breeze—and hence the palace's name—"Palace of the Wind." The upper levels can only be reached by ramps.

LEFT: Pushkar is famous for holding the world's biggest camel fair every October–November (specifically for the full moon day of Kartik). The colorful festival which includes camel races and cattle auctions. Pushkar contains the only temple in India dedicated to Brahma. It is also one of the five *dhams* (pilgrimages) that Hindus aspire to make—the others are Badrinath, Puri, Rameswaram, and Dwarka.

ABOVE: A doorway stands beneath oriel windows within the facade of a house painted the traditional indigo in Jodhpur's Walled city. The color was originally an indication that the building was the home of a follower of a Jodhpuri Brahmin but it also came to be believed that the color wards off mosquitoes.

PAGE 68–69: Near Sikandra is the Mausoleum of Akbar, designed by Akbar himself in a mixture of Muslim, Hindu, and Christian styles. The work was completed by his son Jahangar in 1613. The tomb sits in the middle of a lush high-walled garden which is divided into four equal parts, each with its own gateway. The gateways are 70ft high and made of carved red sandstone and large marble mosaic decorations.

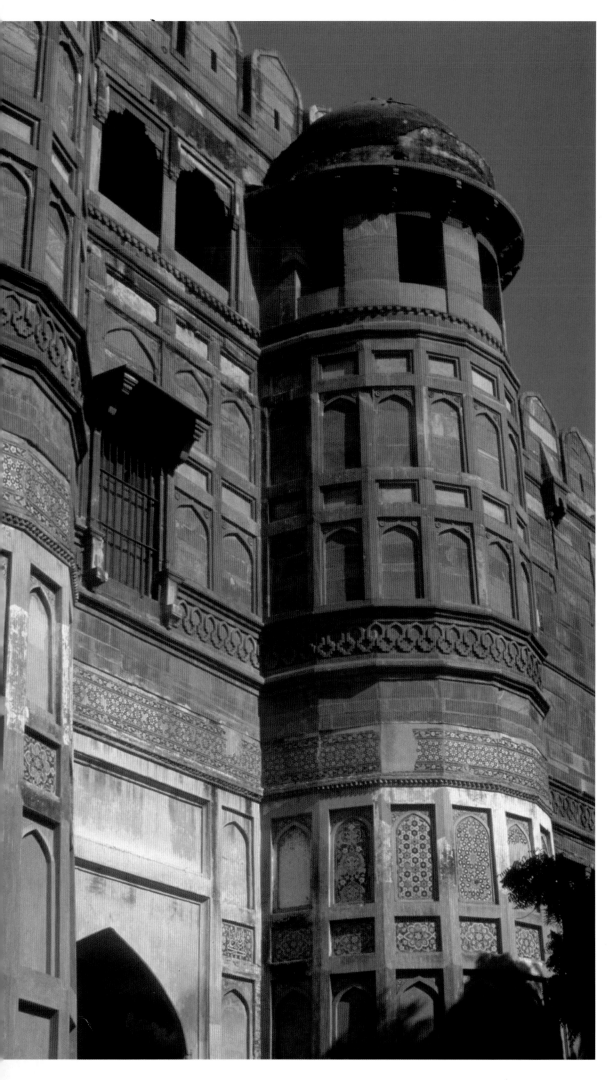

LEFT: Akbar's great fortress at Agra in Uttar Pradesh was built in 1565–71. The massive sandstone gateway stands 72 ft high and is decorated with colorful ceramic tiles. The fortress walls enclose palaces and buildings such as the Moti Masjid (Pearl Mosque) and the Jahangir Mahal where Shah Jahan was imprisoned by his son.

BELOW: Sunset over Agra Fort. The red sandstone citadel ramparts run for almost a mile and a half high above a bend in the river Yamuna and almost a mile from the Taj Mahal. Built by Akbar between 1565 and 1573 it became the great stronghold of the Moghul empire.

LEFT: Panch Mahal at Fatehpur Sikri. The deserted royal city of Fatehpur Sikri was for about 30 years the capital of the Mugal empire until lack of sufficient water for the increasing population forced the move to Agra in 1600. Fatehpur Sikri was founded by Jala-ud-Din Akbar, the third Mughal ruler of India, to celebrate the much desired birth of his son and heir Prince Salim in August 1569. Prince Salim was later to become Emperor Jahangir.

LEFT: The city of Varanasi (formerly Benares) stands on the banks of the River Ganga (Ganges) and is the most important and sacred pilgrimage destination for Hindus who come here in their thousands to worship at the shrine of Lord Kasi Viswanatha. Bathing in the Ganga is believed to wash away sins, and furthermore, by dying here in the holy city rebirth is avoided. This means that believers are liberated from the cycle of life and death. Recently the historic practice of cremating corpses on the banks of the Ganga and then throwing the remains into the river has been banned in an attempt to reduce water pollution.

PAGE 74–75: Pilgrims have made their way to Varanasi (Benares) since time immemorial and consequently it has always been a place of great learning and importance and features prominently in many ancient legends. Temples and shrines are found all over the city but especially beside the river. One of the most important temples is dedicated to the Kaasi Visweswara which enshrines one of the twelve Jyotirlingams of Shiva. Thousands of worshippers journey there to perform an abhishekam—the ceremony of ablutions and symbolic offerings—with water taken from the Ganga river. At the same time mantras are chanted to invoke blessings and inspire spirituality. Millions of pilgrims converge on Varanasi particularly at Shivaratri in the month of Aquarius for the biggest festival of the year.

ABOVE: The Malviya road and rail bridge crosses the River Ganga at Varanasi. It was originally called Dufferin Bridge and built in 1882 as a single bridge with a road running alongside the railroad tracks. The bridge was radically altered in 1847 when it was transformed into a double-decker with the road on the upper level. The Diesel Locomotive Works of Indian Railways—one of the largest locomotive manufacturers in the world—is based in Varanasit.

RIGHT: Marigold flowers and other items for sale at a Varanasi market. Called *puja* (offerings) they will be used during one of the numerous festivals.

FAR RIGHT: One of the tourist attractions of Varanasi is the Sinking Temple which gently subsides into the River Ganga every time it is rebuilt.

ABOVE: The Great Gateway to the Taj Mahal was built in 1648 and is made from red sandstone inscribed with passages from the Quran. The dazzling white marble for the mausoleum came from relatively nearby—a quarry at Makrana near Jodhpur. However the twenty-eight different types of precious and semiprecious stones with which it is elaborately inlaid came from all points of the compass: amethyst from Persia, agate from the Yemen, jasper from Punjab, lapis lazuli from Ceylon and Afghanistan, malachite from Russia, mother of pearl from the Indian Ocean, chrysolite from Egypt, crystal and jade from China, turquoise from Tibet, and diamonds from Golconda.

RIGHT: Emperor Shah Jahan was devastated when his favorite (and second) wife Mumtaz Mahal (meaning "Chosen of the Palace") died bearing him their fourteenth child in 1629. Shah Jahan locked himself away for a week after the shock of her death. When he emerged his hair had turned prematurely gray and he had visibly aged. The kingdom was ordered into mourning for two years. The tomb of Arjumand Banu Begum (Mumtaz Mahal) lies in a basement vault deep within the Taj Mahal. The 99 names of Allah are inscribed on her tomb and the entire sepulcher is elaborately decorated with semiprecious stones. Shah Jahan's tomb lies nearby. He intended to have his own mausoleum but it was never built—the Taj Mahal had already proved far too costly.

LEFT: One of the most beautiful and recognizable buildings in the world— the Taj Mahal at Agra India. The Taj Mahal sits in a magnificent formal four-acre garden which has now been restored to its former glory as it was originally intended when designed by one of Shah Jehan's courtiers, Ali Mardan Khan as an evocation of the gardens of paradise. The lakes and fountains are supplied with water from the river Jamuna via reservoirs; originally the water was moved by bullocks but electricity is now used. The principal long water runs through a red sandstone channel flanked by rows of cypress trees that lead the view up to the mausoleum. The still waters give a perfectly symmetrical reflection of the Taj Mahal.

PAGE 82–83: A distant view of the Taj Mahal through reed beds. At different times of day the Taj changes color as the marble takes on different tones. Under the blaze of the midday sun it dazzles while at dawn and sunset it looks magical in the half light, however at night under the Moon and stars it can look coldly magnificent.

LEFT: A banyan tree in Corbett National Park. The Banyan or Indian fig tree (*Ficus bangaliensis*) can grow enormous. It sends down shoots from its branches which become new trunks and so can spread out over a considerable area. The park is named after Jim Corbett one of the founders of the reserve (India's first) in 1936. The park covers some 200 square miles over the foothills of Kumaun but visitors are only allowed around the fringes of the reserve so as not to disturb the wildlife. In 1973 the park became the first designated Project Tiger Reserve.

ABOVE: Two more views of the exquisite Taj Mahal which probably designed by Ustad Isa Khan Effendi, a Persian from Shiraz, while the dome designed by Ismail Khan.

PAGE 86–87: The 21,890ft high Meru peak seen from Tapovan in the Garhwal Region of India. The Himalaya range is where the Ganga (Ganges) and Yamuna rivers have their source. The area is a place of pilgrimage and many ancient shrines are found in the region. When the snows have melted—between May and November—streams of *yatris* (pilgrims) make their way into the high mountains to visit the temples of Badrinath, Kedarnath, Gangotri, and Yumnotri.

LEFT: In many districts of Arunachal Pradesh, especially along the border with Assam, there is still widespread felling of hardwood trees. Only trained elephants are nimble and strong enough to haul the heavy tree trunks from the forest to a clearing where the trees are loaded on to heavy trucks to be transported and sold.

PAGE 90–91: High up in a deep valley in the Himalayas and only 25 miles south of the border with Tibet lies Badrinath Temple, one of Hinduism's holiest sites. Badrinath means "Lord of the Berries" and the temple was founded in the ninth century by Shankara since when a ramshackle township has grown up around it. Every May after the snows have melted the wooden temple is repainted and then opened to the thousands of worshipers who pilrimage here in the summer. The temple, Badri Narayan, is dedicated to Vishnu who once made his penance in the mythical forest of Badrivan (the Forest of Berries) that once covered the nearby mountains. Inside the temple sitting in a lotus position is a black stone figure of Badri Vishal, which it is strictly forbidden to photograph.

LEFT: Yellow wheel of life sculpture on the roof of Lamayuru Gompa in Ladakh.

RIGHT: Pensi La Glacier in Zanskar Valley, Ladakh. From here the river Stod (or Doda) flows southeast helping to form the River Zanskar that meets the Indus at Nimmu. Zanskar itself is mountain-locked by the Great Himalayan divide and the Zanskar range. It is the remotest part of Ladakh that can be reached by road and is one of the coldest inhabited parts of the globe. The passes can be blocked with snow for seven months of the year and Pensi La can be snowbound in August.

BELOW: Elysium Hill in the town of Shimla on the southern slopes of the Himalayas became the favorite summer resort of the British Raj who came here to escape the blistering heat of cities like Calcutta.

Eastern and Northeastern India

PAGE 94–95: Calcutta Racecourse with the white marble dome of the Voictoria Memorial in the distance. rises between the city tower blocks beyond the trees surrounding the racecourse.

LEFT: In Bihar at Bodh Gaya sits a 82ft high stone effigy of Buddha. Bodh Gaya is the most important pilgrimage site for international Buddhism because this is where Buddha reached enlightenment after years of penance. Around the town are many temples, shrines and monasteries representing many Buddhist nations. The Giant Buddha was consecrated by the Dalal Lama in 1989.

LEFT: Aerial view of the ruins of the monks' cells at Bihar Nalanda University—founded in the fifth century A.D. by Guptas, one of the world's first universities and an important Buddhist center until it was sacked by Afghan invaders in the 12th century. The ruins of eleven monasteries remain here; most of them with thick red brick walls and are aligned north to south, with the entrance to the west and the shrine room to the east. In the center is an open courtyard edged with a verandah off which are small cells for the monks.

ABOVE: Aerial view of the flooded village of Dharbhanga, Bihar. Such dramatic flooding is a constant threat in the great flood plain areas of the sub continent where heavy rainfall can quickly lead to rivers bursting their banks.

The Sikh temple of Har Mandir Sahib in Patna, Bihar, was built to honor the birthplace in 1660 of the tenth and most militant Sikh guru, Guru Gobind Singh, and is the second of the four holiest Sikh shrines. Patna itself is one of the oldest cities in India dating from the sixth century B.C. and in its time has been the center of the Magadhan and Mauryan empires.

The imposing Victoria Memorial building in Calcutta came from a desire by Lord Curzon to celebrate the British Empire. It was designed in a hybrid Italianate-Moghul style by Sir William Emerson and was completed in 1921. On top of the central dome stands a revolving 16ft bronze figure of Victory. The building is faced with white Makrana marble from Jodhpur and sits in splendor in formal gardens that are a very popular meeting and greeting spot for locals in the cool of the evening.

ABOVE: Founded by the East India Company in 1690 around three small fishing villages, one of which was Kalikata, Calcutta became a thriving port thanks to the River Hooghly, a tributary of the River Ganga. However, today the river is badly silted up and large ships can no longer make their way up river.

RIGHT: Colorful film posters hang above a row of shops in Calcutta.

FAR RIGHT: Howrah Bridge crosses the River Hooghly linking Calcutta and the town of Howrah. Over two million people cross this bridge every day. It is usually so crowded that people have to queue to get across.

PAGE 104–105: A suspension foot-bridge in Arunachal Pradesh. Tucked high in the Himalayas in India's extreme northeast, Arunachal Pradesh is another area culturally closer to Tibet than India proper. The area is claimed by China, but armed confrontation is unlikely despite past hostilities.

LEFT: A relief carving of the Hindu elephant-headed god Ganesh at Bhubaneswar, the state capital of Orissa. Ganesh is the son of Shiva and is the popular god of good fortune and learning. He is short and pot-bellied (and often painted yellow, although not here), with one tusk and four hands in which he holds a water lily, a club, a shell, and a discus. He is sometimes shown riding a rat or has one as a companion.

RIGHT: Ancient Buddhist relics under a banyan tree. The famous stone sculptors of Orissa still use the same skills—and claim to use many of the same tools—as their ancient sculpting ancestors.

BELOW: Near Puri stands the Konarak (or Konark) Sun Temple, a masterful example of medieval Orissan architecture and a UNESCO World Heritage Site. Its carvings include polished courtiers, heavenly damsels and some spectacularly erotic scenes drawn from the Kama Sutra. This carved Solar Wheel dates from around 1240, and is one of twenty-four stone wheels adorning the Temple of the Sun at Konarka.

PAGE 108–109: Dzongri Ridge in Sikkim is part of a remote high altitude track that runs between Yoksum and Dzongri which passes near the world's third largest peak, Mount Kanchenjunga (Kanchendzonga). Popular with walkers in the summer the trail principally used by yak herders to move their animals through the mountains.

PAGE 110–111: Terraced rice fields at Ranipool, east Sikkim. Sikkim in the eastern Himalayas had the distinction of being an independent monarchy until 1975. The country was ruled by *Chogyal* (kings) of Tibetan origin from the 1200s. Sikkim is sandwiched between Bhutan to the east, China to the north, and Nepal to the west. The population is largely Nepali-speaking. Sikkim became an Indian protectorate in 1947, and then joined the Union in 1975 following a plebiscite.

LEFT: The old road from Tibet to Sikkim runs through the Yumthang Valley on India.

ABOVE LEFT, ABOVE, AND PAGE 114–115: Views of snow-covered Mount Kanchenjunga. At 28,169ft it is the third highest mountain in the world.

Western India

PAGE 116–117: Gujarat is the wealthiest state in India, thanks in part to its western location on the Arabian Sea. One of the most spectacular sites is the Jain complex of Shatrunjaya Tirtha, an assembly of 108 temples and 872 small shrines spread over nine hilltops.

FAR LEFT: There are a number of Hindu temples in Goa.

LEFT: Detail of north Torana at the Great Stupa at Sanchi. It dates from sometime between the first century B.C. and the first century A.D.

BELOW: The Portuguese controlled Goa for 450 years during which time they built a such buildings as the Church of Our Lady of the Rosary in Old Goa (Velha Goa).

LEFT: There are many interesting temples in Goa with almost every village having its own Hindu temple. These buildings differ from other Indian temples in their architecture and spaciousness. Many of them are centuries old and may well have originally begun as Buddhist shrines.

RIGHT: Monkeys are protected in Indian temples as the representatives of the deity Hanuman. In the Ramayana Lord Hanuman is Rama's chief and most faithful ally in the fight against the demon king of Lanka. He is the god of power and strength and is often shown sitting or bowing at the feet of Rama and Sita. Hanuman has a round red face with sharp white fangs on top of a short thick neck. He has an impressive mane and tail and can, as the need arises, make himself as small as a fly or as big as a mountain. He is usually clasping a mace; his sacred day is Tuesday, and he is the preferred deity of wrestlers.

RIGHT: The Church and Convent of St. Monica started construction on Holy Hill, west of Goa in about 1598 and work continued until completion in 1627 by the Archbishop Dom Aleixo de Menezes. It was destroyed by fire in 1636 but immediately rebuilt. The nunnery contains a large square inner courtyard around which runs a cloistered verandah, off which are numerous halls and cells. At one time the convent contained eleven chapels as well as a novitiate and a seminary for girls. It is still the largest nunnery in Goa and is home to the Mater dei Institute for nuns. The church is dedicated to St. Mary, the façade, in renaissance-style, carries a statue of Our Lady.

PAGE 124–125: On the north coast of Goa lies Anjuna Beach, one time major destination on the hippy trail. On Wednesdays the famous flea market attracts hundreds of people for clothes, jewelery, street food, fruit and vegetables, spices, cameras, drink—generally souvenirs of all descriptions—and entertainment. Haggling is required to ensure a bargain.

LEFT: About five miles from the port of Vasco de Gama in Goa lies the broad, flat and open Oberoi Bogmalo Beach. A former fishing village it is now a holiday resort.

BOTTOM LEFT: Panaji (Panjim) became the capital of Goa in 1843 when the port at Old Goa silted up. The town sits at the mouth of the River Mandovi and has a very European air thanks to its legacy of old Portuguese colonial houses.

BELOW: On a high hill opposite Panaji on the north bank of the River Mandovi is Reis Magos Fort dedicated to the Three Magi kings. It was built in 1551 by Don Alfonso de Noronha to guard the narrow river entrance to Old Goa and overlooks a sandy shoreline on the coast. In its time it has served as a residence for the viceroys of India, before being converted to become a fortress.

PAGE 128–129: Palm trees meet a stretch of golden sand at Anjuna Beach, on the coast of Goa. In the 1960s this was an idyllic hippy haven where peace, quiet, and the simple life on a sunny beach were the great attraction.

RIGHT: Goa is now the twenty-fifth state of the Indian Union following its days as a Portuguese colony and is one of the most popular beach holiday destinations in India. The easy tropical climate means that there are many idyllic beaches all the way along the coast.

ABOVE: One of the hundreds of white marble Jain temples on the holy hill of Shatrunjaya, located near Palitana. Jainism was founded in India in about the sixth century B.C. by the sage Mahavira. Jains do not believe in a creator god, but rather live to perfect human nature through a monastic and ascetic life.

LEFT: Female tiger resting in a cave in Bandhavgarh National Park, Madhya Pradesh. The park boasts the highest density of tigers in all Indian reserves.

RIGHT: Temple at Khajuraho, Madhya Pradesh. Built by the Chandella kings between the tenth and twelfth centuries, the temples here are smothered with beautifully sculpted erotic carvings.

RIGHT: The stone stupas at Sanchi in Madhya Pradesh date from between the first century B.C. and the first century A.D. making them some of the earliest religious structures in India. Although Sanchi has no known connection with Buddha himself the hemispherical buildings (stupas) were built as funerary mounds to hold holy relics of Buddha and his followers but the stupas acquired a sacred veneration of their own for Buddhists. The stupas are surrounded by shrines, temples, commemmorative columns, and monasteries. The complex was rescued from being smothered by the jungle and restoration started in 1912.

PAGE 136–137: Mallinath Temple is part of the Jain temple complex on top of Mount Girnar and dominates the town of Junagadh in Gujarart. The marble temple and four other Jain temples date from the twelfth century. Junagadh is an interesting and ancient city which was from the fourth century B.C. until around 232 B.C. the capital of western Gujarat when it was ruled by the Buddhist Mauryas.

LEFT: One of the highlights of Gujarat is the Ranjit Vilas Palace at Wankaner, a sumptuous architectural mix of Indo-Victorian Gothic-Venetian-Rajput styles designed by the Maharaja of Wankaner himself and built between 1899 and 1914. The garage houses a royal collection of automobiles, including a 1921 Rolls-Royce Silver Ghost. Part of the palace is now a hotel.

PAGE 140–141: Once staffed entirley by women and built to catch the cool southwest breeze in the summer the Jahaz Mahal, or the Ship's Palace is generally considered to be one of the most elegant and romantic palaces in India. It is located between two lakes and is part of the massive royal fortress complex of Mandu. The building dates from around the late fifteenth century and was probably commissioned by Ghiyas al-Din (about 1469–1500) who was rumored to have 15,000 women in his harem. He also had a personal bodyguard of 500 young and beautiful Abyssinian and Turkish women who were dressed as men.

PAGE 142–143: A bend in a river near Kanha Meadows in Kanha National Park, Madhya Pradesh. The reserve is home to hundreds of species of animal and birds which roam in its 772 square miles of hills, deciduous forests, savannah, and grasslands.

BELOW AND RIGHT: Deep in the semiarid hills of the Deccan in Maharashtra lies a remarkable complex of caves carved into the rock sides of a horseshoe-shaped ravine. Ajunta's twenty-eight colonnaded caves were known to locals, but only became known to the outside world in 1819 when a local scout indicated the site to British soldiers. Until then the caves entrances had been hidden by dense foliage. Inside the caves were extraordinary carvings and paintings which were made by itinerant Buddhist monks when they founded their first permanent monasteries here. Excavations have dated the earliest caves to the second century B.C. At its peak over 200 monks lived in the complex alongside a small army of laborers, painters, and sculptors. But at some time in the seventh cewntury the site was mysteriously abandoned and was soon forgotten by everyone—a vital reason why the caves and their treasures have remained so remarkably intact and undamaged.

PAGE 146–147: Victoria Station, Mumbai (Bombay). Both the ornate Victoria railway station which was and the red double decker buses illustrate British influence on Mumbai—so much so in fact, that the scene could almost be in Britain.

LEFT: Relief sculpture showing Shiva dancing in an elephant skin. The story illustrates Shiva in a wrathful manifestation, an appropriate relief to guard the entrance to Dhumar Lena, Ellora Cave 29.

ABOVE: **The lights of** Mumbai (Bombay) at twilight prove the city's boast that it is the most dynamic and westernized city in India. Over 13 million people live here. Although the port handles half of India's foreign trade, Mumbai is most famous for being the home of the world's largest movie-making industry—Bollywood.

RIGHT: Posters for Bollywood movies. Around 750 full length feature films a year are made here, predominently in Hindi.

LEFT, PAGES 152–153, AND 154–155: In Maharashtra lie the remarkable caves at Ellora. Dating as far back as 600 A.D., there are 34 Hindu, Jain, and Buddhist caves at Ellora which are considered some of the finest caves in India although not as old as those at Ajunta. The caves are nearby the old caravan route between the ports on the west coast and the prosperous northern cities. Excavations show that occupation started in the sixth century—at much the same time as Ajanta was abandoned—and continued for the next 500 years. Ellora did not escape the iconoclastic destructions of the Muslims in the thirteenth century but thanks to the hard rock the damage was relatively minimal. Kalash Temple in Cave 16 is the largest and most impressive of the Ellora caves. A lump of solid basalt is the world's largest monolith and has been cut into a series of interconnected halls, galleries, and shrines. It was carved to be a recreation of Shiva and Parvati's Himalayan home, Mount Kailash, the divine axis between heaven and earth. Originally the temple was coated with brilliant white lime plaster to give it the appearance of a snowy mountain.

RIGHT: Dozens of lotus-gathering elephants hold up a huge raised platform on which sits a 95ft high *shikhara* (pyramid tower) in Kalash Temple at Ellora.

Southern India

PAGE 156–157: Uninhabited Jolly Buoy Island is one of the Andaman islands and is part of Wandoor National Marine Park. The seas around here contain some of the finest coral reefs which are home to exotically colorful fish, many of them unique to the area.

LEFT AND RIGHT: Closeup detail and long-distance views of the Sri Padmanabhaswamy Temple. Situated inside the East Fort at Thiru-vananthapuram (formerly Trivandrum) the captial of Kerala, is the Sri Padmanabhaswamy Temple. The temple is designed in Dravidian style (usually found in Tamil Nadu) with a seven-tier gateway and is closed to non-Hindus. Inside is a long corridor with 324 beautifully carved stone pillars. The temple is dedicated to Vishnu in the form of Lord Padmanabha. He is enshrined here in eternal sleep. Worshipers offer him coconut shells filled with rice to commemorate one of the appearances of the god. A number of shrines to others deities are also located around the temple complex. Lord Padmanabha appears on the last day of two ten-day festivals, Meenam (in spring) and Thulam (in fall), when he is brought out into the sunshine and taken to the nearby shores of the Arabian Sea where he is ceremonially dipped in the water before returning to his shrine.

PAGE 160–161: The Alleppey canals in Kerala.

RIGHT: The state of Kerala is on the far southwest tip of India. It has a tropical monsoon climate and contains forty-one rivers and numerous lakes and waterways making traveling by water the easiest and best way to explore the country. Kerala is one of the less modernized regions of India but nevertheless full of fascinating history and traditions. There are fewer ancient buildings here because the main structures are historically made of wood and so most of the ancient buildings have disappeared over time.

PAGE 164–165: One of the glories of Kerala is its wonderful coastline with beaches along much of its 342 miles.

ABOVE AND RIGHT: Keralan Kathakali dancer. Kathikali is the great dance drama of southern India, taught at the famous Keralan Kalamandalam academy. The dance has its roots in the temple dramas enacted for the kings and Brahmin caste of the state of Kerala and it is as old as Hinduism itself—although it gained its current form in the seventeenth century. The dances are performed on stages with no props, scenery, or dialog: the actors tell their stories through gestures, eye movements, and highly elaborate costumes.

PAGE 168–169: The former palace of the Maharaja of Mysore, Amba Vilas, sits in the center of Mysore and is one of the largest palaces in India. It was built in 1912 on the site of the former palace which had burned down a few years earlier. The palace was designed in Indo-Saracenic style by Henry Irwin, (British consultant architect for Madras) for the 24th Wadiyar Raja. For special occasions the palace is illuminated by 5,000 lightbulbs.

ABOVE AND RIGHT: Kerala, on the Arabian Sea, is a union of three regions—Travancore (Thiruvithamcoore), Cochin, and Malabar. The state's main language is Malayam, with a significant Tamil population also. Kochi (Cochin), the capital and main port, has over a million people. Built on a cluster of islands, it was a mainstay of the spice trade. Trading links brought influences from all quarters—the Dutch ruled here briefly, and the Synagogue of 1568 was decorated with Chinese tilework. The area has many aquatic attractions, including Koyalam Beach and the Allappuzha (Alleppey) canals.

About forty miles south of Kochi, Allappuzha has the nickname the "Venice of the East," something it shares with almost every city in Asia that has a canal. Unlike its competitors, Allappuzha lives up to its name, for life here is entirely supported by its riverine network. Farming is wet-rice cultivation. Spectacular houseboats scud gently across the lakes, lagoons, and rivers. The state capital, Thiruvananthapuram, is an important IT center. The Vikram Sarabhai Space Centre is located on the outskirts, and it saw its first launch in 1966. Many people call the city by its traditional name, Trivandrum. These photographs show the coastal area, particularly Samudra beach.

LEFT AND ABOVE LEFT: Two more views of the Keralan coast.

ABOVE: Bowls of dyes for sale at Devaraja market near Mysore, India.

PAGE 174: The Vivekananda memorial at Kanyakumari, in Tamil Nadu stands on the most southerly tip of the Indian Peninsula where the Arabian Sea, the Indian Ocean, and the Bay of Bengal meet. Over 400 yards out to sea on a rocky islet is the memorial to Swami Vivekananda, the Bengali religious leader, philosopher, and social reformer.

PAGE 175: Intricate carvings cover the Kapaleeshwara Temple in Madras.

173

PAGE 176–177: The Vivekananda memorial at Kanyakumari was built in 1970 by the Vivekananda Rock Memorial Committee to commemorate the visit of Swamy Vivekananda here in December 1892, for deep meditation and enlightenment. The memorial designed by Sthapati Sri S.K. Achari and consecrated by Srimad Swami Vireshwarananda, President of Ramakrishna mission was formally inaugurated by Sri. V.V. Giri, the then President of India in September 1970. The memorial as a whole has two main structures Vivekananda Mandapam and Sripada Mandapam, on two rocks standing adjacent to each other separated by about 200 yards. The smaller rock known as "Sripada Parai" has been revered as a sacred place even from very ancient times. Legend says that Goddess Kanya Kumari meditated on this rock and there is actually a projection on the rock similar in form to a human foot believed to be the "Sripadam" or the feet of the Goddess. It is the focal point of the memorial. It is now enclosed in a square shrine or Sripada Madapam. This shrine consists of the sanctum sanctorum, an inner compartment as well as outer compartment. There is an outer platform all around.

LEFT: Not far from the Kumari Amman Temple is the Gandhi Mandapam, constructed at the spot where the urn containing the ashes of Mahatma Gandhi was kept for public view before a portion of its contents was immersed in the three seas. (Arabian Sea, the Indian Ocean, and the Bay of Bengal) It resembles an Oriyan temple and was designed so that on Gandhiji's birthday (October 2), the sun's rays fall on the place where his ashes were kept.

PAGE 180-181 AND ABOVE: Tamil Nadu—"Land of the Tamils"—is a state at the southern tip of India, formerly part of the Madras state (renamed in August 1968). It is known for its rich tradition of literature, music, and dance, and is one of the most progressive and industrialized states in India. Its major industry produces textiles, and the city of Tirupur—the "textile valley of India"—is the largest garment exporter in the country.

ABOVE: Alleppey canal and palms.

RIGHT: Silver Oak islands in among the tea near Munnar in the Western Ghats. This mountain range runs along the western coast of India, from the Vindhya-Satpura ranges in the north to the southern tip.

PAGE 184: Keralan Mosque.

PAGE 185: Ganesha Ratha Temple in Mamallapuram.

LEFT AND PAGE 186–187: Seven miles west of Hyderabad in the state of Andhra Pradesh lies one of the most impressive fortresses in India. Almost 400ft high up on a solid granite hill Fort Golconda was the capital of the seventh Qutb Shahi kings (who originated from Persia), from 1518 until the late sixteenth century. The earliest parts of the fort date from the early thirteenth century although the biggest portion was built in the sixteenth and seventeenth centuries. Its gates are studded with gigantic iron spikes to prevent elephants from battering them down. The six mile long outer wall punctuated with 87 semi-circular bastions protects four separate forts as well as temples, mosques, and palaces.

RIGHT: One of the most ancient heritage sites in India is the temple complex town of Madurai in Tamil Nadu where the Meenakshi Sundareswarar temple towers above the surrounding landscape. According to legend, this is the spot where the wedding of Shiva and Meenakshi took place. Thousands of Hindus make pilgrimage to the temples in particular to worship the fish-eyed (in other word beautiful) goddess Meenakshi.

PAGE 190-191: Just north of Muthuppettai lies Kovilur Temple sacred to Hindus who worship the deity Mantrapureeswarar (Shiva) here. Hindu men ritually bathe in the temple pools where according to legend the deities Rama, Lakshmanan, Jambavan, Sugreevan, and Hanuman stopped to worship while on their way to Sri Lanka.

Page 192: The Gandhi Mandapam, see also pages 178–179.